ON THE SHRED OF A
CLOUD

ON THE SHRED
OF A
CLOUD

Notes in a Travel Book

by

Rolf Edberg

Translated by Sven Åhman

UNIVERSITY OF ALABAMA PRESS
University, Alabama

Translator's Note

Thanks are due the American–Scandinavian Foundation, in New York, for permission to quote a portion of the fifty-seventh stanza of the Icelandic poem Voluspá as it appears in H. A. Bellows' translation of the Poetic Edda, published by the Foundation in 1923. All biblical quotations are from the King James Version.

Sven Åhman

Translated into English from **Spillran av ett Moln,**
Copyright © 1966 by Rolf Edberg
Published by P. A. Norsted & Söners Förlag
Stockholm, Sweden

*English translation copyright © 1969
by University of Alabama Press*

Standard Book Number: 8173–6610–5
Library of Congress Catalog Card Number: 76–89989

Manufactured in the United States of America

Contents

To Jörgen, *traveling companion*

"There is only one heroism in the world: to see the world as it is and to love it."
—Romain Rolland

i

Author's Preface to the English Translation

In the years that have elapsed since the autumn of 1966, when this book was first published in Scandinavia, hardly a day has passed without our attention being drawn to some new evidence of the increasingly precarious condition of man's natural environment. The alarms are being sounded every day in our newspapers . . .

—In one of them we read of traffic policemen in some parts of downtown Tokyo having to return to their precincts to inhale oxygen after only half an hour on duty. In another paper we see pictures of Japanese school children at play in Yokkaichi; they are wearing face-masks that filter the city's filthy air through purifying chemicals as they breathe.

—On another day, a dispatch from New York City tells us that contamination of the air with carbon monoxide has already reached a level that may well be threatening the brain functions of man. A former mayor of the same city says it is wallowing in "a sewer of polluted air."

—On yet another day, a well-known American meteorologist warns that the time may soon come when air pollution will overtake the self-purifying power of the air, permitting a lethal smog to envelop the earth and slowly smother human civilization.

—Then there was that memorable day a few months ago when the once-proud Cuyahoga River, flowing sluggishly into Lake Erie, was officially declared a "fire hazard"—its waters are so polluted with flammable oil. Each and every day, the story goes on, Lake Erie receives from various sources in five states no less than a billion and a half gallons of sewerage and more than nine and a half billion gallons of industrial waste.

The list of such disturbing proofs of man's criminal abuse of nature could be extended almost without end.

But the very accumulation of alarming reports, especially those appearing in the popular press, has given rise to a growing public awareness of the environmental aspect of the human predicament. It is being recognized by more and more people in many parts of the world that man's very existence as a species of life is in jeopardy. Demands for prompt and effective action to put a stop to the further needless contamination of water and air and soil are becoming more numerous and more vehement all the time. We can foresee the day when the problem of man's natural environment will be recognized as by far the most important of all *social* problems—locally, regionally, nationally, and internationally.

In my own country such problems of the environment are already considered pre-eminent, and they are being widely discussed in the popular press, over the airwaves, and in parliamentary bodies. As governor of a Swedish province, I have these problems before me every day. Sweden was the first country in the world to create a special state agency for the protection of the environment, and that agency has been given very wide-ranging powers. And at the United Nations General Assembly in the fall of 1968, it was Sweden that spearheaded a resolution demanding international action to put a stop to the further destruction of the human environment. In a rare moment of unanimity, after only a day of debate, the General Assembly voted to call a world conference on the problem of the environment, to be held in 1972. This may mark the start of the kind of global ap-approach to these questions which this book was—and is— asking for.

Another hopeful step was taken in the spring of 1969, when Sweden became the first country in the world to ban the use of DDT and its derivatives for any purpose whatsoever. This action was of more than national import, having been undertaken as part of an international effort to discover whether local prohibition will reduce the amount of DDT finding its way into plants and animals (including man). A hopeful step, but little more than that. The ban in Sweden —voluntarily the guinea-pig country in an international experiment—will reduce the world's total use of DDT by only seven hundred tons annually—very little by comparison with, for example, the approximately eleven thousand tons of this poison that were used last year in the United States alone. However, restrictions on the use of DDT and similiar chemicals have already been imposed in a number of western countries, including the United States (some of the fifty states are now considering banning DDT entirely), and there is reason to expect this trend to continue.

Even so, the poisoning of his environment is only part of the threat to man's future. The accelerating destruction of the environment and the pillage of the natural resources of the globe must always be considered against the backdrop of the soaring increase in the world's population— since this book was written it has grown by another several hundred million, and the rate of growth has risen. Furthermore, all these developments are taking place in a world where the arms race continues in the shadow of the nuclear bomb.

Thus, I venture to think that this little book is as topical now as it was when first published several years ago. It attempts to do something more than merely describe the present threats to our environment. Anyone who tries to find out what is really happening to our changed and changing world is confronted by an imposing body of literature embracing many specialized fields of knowledge. Even if one can find time to read the major works in each field, there is a further difficulty in grasping the interrelationships among the diverse discoveries and concepts with which they deal. In this book I have tried to weave many of the strands into a coherent pattern, one that may afford other laymen such as myself a fairly wide perspective on the human condition within the dizzying totality of time and space.

This sounds a bit pretentious, I admit. In defense, I can only say that I began to write largely for the purpose of clarifying certain concepts in my own mind. I may also have had a feeling that the musings of a father might be something worth passing on to his hiking companion on so many treks in the Scandinavian mountains—as worthwhile a legacy to one's son as the material things one leaves behind. It was only later that I decided to publish what had been started as rather personal notes. The surprisingly large number of letters that I have received since then from readers in all walks of life have given me a feeling that perhaps my book has, after all, given voice to some of the concern about the future that so many people feel today.

Now that the University of Alabama Press has ventured to publish an English version of the book, I am of course wondering how these "travel notes," with their pronounced Scandinavian background, will be received by American readers. I am quite aware, of course, that the United States, with its high standard of living and its important position in the world, feels the impact of the problems dealt with in this book more strongly than most countries do—and aware, also, that the United States has enormous resources that could be mobilized in the struggle to deal with those problems in a realistic and effective manner.

Karlstad, Sweden   *Rolf Edberg*
June, 1969

ON THE SHRED
OF A
CLOUD

I

*". . . as if the cosmic
realms of death were not enough . . ."*

WE ARE CLIMBING TOWARDS RUSSHALSEN FROM MEMU-
rubu. Below us lies Gjende, a deep green. The peaks on the
south side are reflected, bluish black, in the water.

My companion walks ahead. There is a swing to his step,
the easy pace of the seventeen-year old. With natural sure-
footedness he moves to the lay of the land. It used to be that
I would lead our hikes and find the suitable paths in the pathless. Now the tables are turned and I have to accept it.

The way up is steep. On the first slopes, my fifty years
make their weight felt in the boots, but things get better after
a while, once you have found the right rhythm. So far, I am
keeping pace with my companion. So far—and perhaps for
another few years.

The sun is blinding, although it is still early morning.
Yesterday, as we trekked toward the mountains, clouds were
dragging far down through the valleys. The light was dull,
and the rain clattered. On the expanse between Bygdin and
Gjende there was newly fallen August snow. This is one of

3

those summers when the low pressures are standing in line, waiting their turn. We braced ourselves for a soggy hike.

But today the sun is shining again, and it feels as if it had never been otherwise and will never be otherwise. The sun glistens on the crests of Besshö and Kollhöin, freshly powdered by yesterday's snowfall. It has already melted the tufts of snow at our level, and water trickles playfully through willow brush and across smooth rocks. It presses sweat from the forehead of the elder of us hikers.

The sun is here and now. Over these mountains. But we look at the angle of its rays and recall that now it is also dawning over the land of the Irish, and that in a little while the first rays will also be reflected in millions of window panes in the man-made termite nests of Manhattan. And so it is going to continue to be as the sun unremittingly shoves the cloak of night around our revolving ball.

And precisely where the cloak is pushed aside, in the land of wandering morning, the miracle occurs all the time— the dew lifts, the flowers unfold, green leaves start up their oxygen factories again, and all manner of living creatures resume the hunt for food. And the song of the birds is awakened.

The song of birds is an essential part of this context. It is coming from some willow brush. There is the redwing fluting its twelve-tone scale. And that chiming sound when the redwing pauses—a sound coming as from brittle bells— can only be that of the bluethroat. He is at the top of his form. The notes trickle like drops of water.

It may be imagination, but I always sense that the song of birds is clearer on a sunny morning after the rain. In the same way as the colors of the landscape seem purer and the scent of the earth stronger.

We are crossing the ridge now. Off and on, my companion stops. He picks an ice ranunculus from the edge of some left-over snow ledge, or a mountain gentian just opened by the sun, blue as if it were a concentrate of all the blueness in the world. Or he points to a ptarmigan cooing away, her wing dragging deceptively to divert attention from her nest and her young. My companion's eye is keen and his mind open, and there is a grave joy in his laconic comments.

I feel a warmth welling up inside me. Perhaps this is what I have been able to pass on to him: the urge to live within and with nature. What better could I have given?

We pause for a moment and wash our lungs with strong, clean air. Behind us and ahead the frozen, choppy mountain sea billows with white foam around the crests, the light playing strongly close by and fading into a blue haze towards the horizons.

By tacit agreement we have stowed our wrist-watches in the rucksacks. They must not chew time to pieces for us. We want to own our time, to make each moment a goal in itself.

At such a moment as this old Linnaeus may come ambling along, delivering a quotation with a casual gesture. He was twenty-five years old when he first visited the Norwegian mountains and jotted down his impressions on scraps of paper, never intending them for publication. And this may be why they have retained their delicate, naive freshness. He had, he wrote, "for some years, thank God, been in reasonable health, although somewhat heavy and poorly qualified." But: "As soon as I got up into the mountains, it was as if I had received new life and been relieved of a heavy burden."

I recognize the symptoms, the gift of the mountains— the feeling of liberation, of nerves coming to rest.

You must not be in a hurry in the mountains. You have to be able to pause like this once in a while, taking in the panorama of playing lines, absorbing the vastness in your soul. Sensing the peace over all the peaks. Listening to the silence. Discovering the same amazement as always that everything is familiar and yet new. You have to be able to shrink yourself into a dwarf in the enormity.

There is solemnity in such a moment.

We continue along Lake Russevatn, reflecting the shiny black pyramid of Gloptind peak. It has the inward feel characteristic of mountain waters on clear, still days.

Then upwards again, along the foaming Blåtjönåi. Turning around, we can see sun and cloud playing over Blåbreen glacier and the Styggebre crest.

This is Jotunheimen, the "home of the giants." The writer Aasmund Vinje so named it. National romanticism, yes—but to the point. There is strength and stature in the name. It conveys a picture of icy peaks far above the busy world of human beings.

Of course, as I walk here and register my impressions in such words as "enormity" and "home of giants" and "exalted peaks," I am measuring with my own yardstick, that of an earthbound man. Subjectively, it is the proper one for me to use. It is the yardstick of my own experience.

Yet the play of the clouds over the glacier can inspire one to turn the perspective around. Then the peaks shrink. The radius of the earth, I recall, is just about four thousand miles. Whether from the highest peaks or from the surface of the sea, the distance to the center of the earth remains about the same. The deviations—deviations that make me think of "enormity"—are minuscule, globally speaking. The distance from the topmost mountain peaks, which I cannot reach, to the surface of the sea, is only about a thousandth part of the radius of the earth.

Even to the astronaut, that brother of the clouds, hurtling around the globe in his capsule at an altitude of a hundred and sixty miles, the lovely valleys and the glistening peaks of the earth have been rolled into one mass without perceptibly varying levels. And yet he, the hero and matinée idol of our day, inflated by official propaganda machines, has been lifted only a little above the surface of the earth. If I tried to plot him on an ordinary desk globe he would not reach much beyond the varnish.

The mountains around me become no less magnificent when I turn the telescope around in this way. But I am groping for something that takes the form of a question: have we not reached the point in time when it is useful, perhaps even necessary, to see ourselves in this double perspective?

There are the blue mountains. Below them a film brushed across the continents, so thin as to make it impossible even for the finest brush to apply its equivalent to any desk globe. At its thickest it is only some fractions of a millionth part of the radius of the earth, But this film is the condition and the domicile of what we mean by organic life. Without it the continents would be sterile moonscapes. Inside this thin covering, in the porous darkness of the soil, bacteria—those tireless and mute servants of life—are busily at work on exhausted organisms, liberating the salts that are the premise of the uninterrupted renewal and circulation of life, of everything that grows and blossoms, of the song of birds, of man himself.

Just below this film is the solid mass of the globe, glowing with black fire in its interior—an abode of death from the point of view of organic life. And if I raise my sight over the mountains, I know that the oxygen filling my lungs, as the plants of the earth fill my stomach, will be rapidly rarefied and soon gone. Outside the ozone covering: a black emptiness, where the cold of space and its radiation, softened by no air cover, join in creating another realm of death.

Here, then, in the paper-thin margin between the black deaths, we love and dream and strive, we indulge in our politics and contemplate our interesting personalities. Here we are sometimes caught up in a solemn zeal of existing, in worship of the beautiful picture nature has painted on the film. Here is the home of mankind—in a narrow frontier, with the hot black death of the globe beneath, the cold black death of space above. A marginal home for marginal beings.

And now, as if the cosmic realms of death on both sides of the thin margin of life were not enough, we are toying with a third death—that of collective suicide.

Did you try to escape from something up here? Did you imagine that you could satiate yourself with the stillness of the wilderness and so put all your other memories and senses to sleep? What an illusion. It is quite impossible to ignore what goes on in the busy world of man beyond a few valleys and blue ridges, a world of which one is a part.

You may walk in your mountains, listen to the silence, and have the sincere feeling that you are receiving "new life," and yet, heavy echoes will be heard penetrating the silence—echoes of those young men in uniform marching around the globe. Yellow, brown, black, and white soldiers, all of them moving in that same robot-like gait.

Marching where?

It is, after all, the way it has always been. Scenes from human history repeating themselves. Friends and foes have changed, but new young men have obediently continued the uniformed march.

Twice in the last generation the march led into world war. The last time, a little corporal with a stubbornly raised arm was the one who got hold of the torch and put it to the powder keg. Soon all the continents, and even the most remote islands in the ocean, were involved in mass slaughter. Men of all colors fought each other on billowing fronts, often not knowing against whom they were fighting, and rarely knowing for what. The women and children of the villages were stricken, homes were blown away. Fifty million people never learned who won—if anybody won. Monuments were erected to a few of the dead; wreaths were laid at the graves of new unknown soldiers; and then it was discovered all of a sudden that one had been fighting the wrong enemies all along! Former enemies now became allies, yesterday's allies became adversaries—and the marching continued. And it continues.

The way it has always been. Except that something new has been added after all—added at the very moment the corporal's war ebbed: a poisonous mushroom towering far above the ramparts of man, above pyramids and skyscrapers, castles, temples—threatening the planet itself.

It towers above the mountains too, above the home of the giants. It casts a shadow over the valley in which we are walking. There is no escaping it—not even in this solitude, brimming with quiet and timeless by human standards.

For we belong to a generation that has crossed an epochal borderline.

In the environment of which he is part, know-it-all man is searching. With his brain and his hands, he seeks to tap the secrets of his marginal home, haunted by unsolved riddles that drive him beyond its borders. The thirst for knowledge is the distinguishing trait of his species. But not all that he finds is without danger for him. The deeper he penetrates into the workshop of nature, the more hazardous the forces he conjures up.

Along the road man travels the slumbering energy of the atom lay waiting to be freed. From the moment a twenty-six year old functionary in the patent office at Berne captured a formula for the unity of the universe from the depths beyond the stars, man held the key to the interior of the atoms in his hand. A few symbols in an equation—$e = mc^2$—wrote the headline for a new age. They said that matter is dormant energy and that matter moving with the speed of light releases its mass and is transformed into energy again. They revealed the amount of energy in every atom nucleus.

It is ironic to reflect on how little awareness scientists had of the effect of the forces they unleashed. To Einstein, the famous formula was the summary of a theory that attempted to capture reality beyond what could be observed. And when Ernest Rutherford first succeeded in splitting the atom, he was only a representative of human curiosity wondering if the hitherto indivisible could be divided. Equally unwitting was Harold Urey when he found the isotope of heavy hydrogen, deuterium; he never supposed that it would have practical application outside the laboratory. Certainly none of them, in their moments of discovery, had any vision of Hiroshima.

But just a quarter of a century after Rutherford's sharp-shooting man succeeded for the first time in transforming matter into energy on a large scale—on that July night at Alamogordo in the New Mexico desert, where the blinding poison mushroom rose skywards and gave an age its picture, just as three letters in an equation had produced its headline. Those who stared, terror-stricken, at the pillar of fire in the desert night, were given reassurances: to detonate an atom bomb takes uranium, and to eradicate humanity would require as much uranium as existed on earth. A few years later the world—with the help of Urey's innocuous isotope—was thrust into the hydrogen age at a secret test in the Pacific. One observer wrote: "It was as if a giant hand had dropped a piece scooped out of the blazing sun." A coral island of an atoll disappeared as the water around it rose in whirls of steam. Man the know-it-all had fingered the primary building block of the universe and succeeded in imitating the processes of the interior of the sun.

It was no sun of peace that rose over the South Sea atoll seven years after the corporal's war ended. "I am scared," cried Urey, when he realized what his isotope could be used for. It was almost like hearing an echo of a certain nineteenth-century fantasy in which the Lord brings the play to an end by declaring, against those who have been intruding too eagerly and too far into His workshop: "Closing-up time, gentlemen!" A fiction had become a possibility. Man had bought his ticket for an opening night on the stage of history that could turn out to be the closing night.

Our marginal home on the thin film between the two black deaths is seemingly much the same as before. But life is not the same. It became something else the moment man acquired the capacity to annihilate himself. Our entire situation became different at that moment, but not our way of thinking.

The threat of annihilation! The mountain wanderer twists and turns the world around, trying to visualize a concrete reality behind it. But how is one to give substance to such visions, when there is no experience to compare them with? Our visions of Hiroshima and Nagasaki are, after all, too limited. For the layman, a destructive force counted in megatons and gigatons becomes something unfathomable and therefore almost unreal.

The scientists are groping, too. Their predictions are most uncertain. As little as they imagined the consequences when they first uncorked the bottle with the genie in it can they now give a clear answer to the question of what would happen if the destructive forces that have been accumulated for a couple of decades by the great powers were actually to be unleashed. But none dares to deny that the annihilation of man by his own hand now looms as a terrifying possibility.

The mountain climber working his way towards the ridge between Hestlaegerhö and Styggehö, with an eagerly prattling brook by his side, attempts some rough, layman's calculations.

The heaviest bomb dropped in Europe during World War II was the blockbuster. It contained roughly one ton of TNT. The atom bomb that killed almost a hundred thousand inhabitants of Hiroshima on their way to work on an August morning in 1945 had an explosive force corresponding to twenty thousand blockbusters. Thus the unleashed forces of the atom, in first blush, had increased the explosive power of a single bomb twenty thousand times.

Yet it was not long before the Hiroshima bomb was being spoken of as old-fashioned. New weaponeers shrugged it off as a "conventional" bomb, so awkward that it could be given the humorous nickname "Fat Man." The superpowers, involved in a hectic race to retain or obtain "superiority" (or at least to catch up with the other fellow's superiority), devoted enormous resources to storing a maximum of destructive force within a minimum of mass. The hydrogen bomb afforded new possibilities. A twenty-megaton hydrogen bomb actually weighs only a ton or so, but it has an explosive force corresponding to twenty million World War II blockbusters. It would correspond—according to calculations in an American report—to a solid pillar of TNT covering six big city blocks to the height of the Empire State Building.

The step from the blockbuster to Hiroshima seemed enormous when it was taken, but it was a minuscule step compared to the one from Hiroshima to the superbomb.

During the period of escalating nuclear tests, when the poison mushroom rose now in the East, now in the West, when countries comprising eight per cent of the population of the world permitted themselves to gamble with the global environment as if it were their private test tube for high explosives, six hundred megatons of nuclear energy were exploded. This meant that in peacetime arms tests two hundred times more explosive energy was detonated than in the five years of World War II.

A single superbomb, such as that fifty-seven megaton monster which was detonated over Arctic areas on one memorable day, corresponded to three thousand Hiroshima bombs. This single bomb had a content of destructive power twenty times that of all bombs exploded during World War II, and six times that released by all projectiles in all wars since the invention of gunpowder.

12

Such a concentration of destructive energy is simply beyond the grasp of concrete imagination. There are memories of moon craters opened by blockbusters where homes or factories had stood. It is barely possible to visualize Hiroshima, since in some way—even though at a distance—we have all experienced it. But when a single bomb multiplies the blockbuster sixty million times, and by itself exceeds all of the roaring, burning inferno of a world war by twenty times, one is in a realm so far removed from all concrete experience as to permit only the haziest notions of its meaning.

There have been experiments with even larger monsters. The megaton unit—the measure of the explosive power in a million tons of TNT—is on its way to becoming too small. There has been talk of gigatons, of the thousand-megaton bomb, which by itself would multiply all the bombs of World War II three hundred thirty-three times. This monstrous lump does not exist yet, but it is more than a nightmare; there is no doubt that it can be built. The crux, for the moment, is how to deliver it.

It has never been revealed publicly just how much explosive energy is now stored in the arsenals of the great powers. There is good reason for an estimate of at least sixty thousand megatons—sixty billion tons of TNT. Thus it can be figured that the amount in storage corresponds, in tonnage, to five hundred times the total weight of the entire population of the world. In all earlier wars taken together, the amount of explosive power used was only about one six-hundredth as much as the amount now in storage. Yet such computations convey little or nothing, really. The pregnancy of megatonnage becomes fully understandable only when distributed among the world's three and a half billion human beings. That makes almost twenty tons per person. Such is your share and mine of the hoarded power of annihilation of the world.

Each of us, yellow, white, or black, young, middle-aged,

or elderly, is sitting on a powder keg corresponding to twenty blockbusters. My individual share is generous, quite enough to blow up a small-sized city.

Of course, megatons are only a rule-of-thumb way of expressing explosive force. Even sixty billion tons of TNT could not be so evenly distributed as to erase all human life. So far as the effects of pressure and explosion are concerned, a fifty-megaton bomb is capable of blowing up all buildings within a radius of some fifteen to twenty miles; it is, in those terms, only a hefty enlargement of the blockbuster.

But the megaton measure says nothing about the far more fatal effects of the bomb. It says nothing, for instance, about the fire-storm that a superbomb could ignite, which would probably be capable of burning an area the size of the whole province around Stockholm, Oslo, or Copenhagen. It says nothing about how the enormous heat at the center of the detonation consumes all oxygen within a wide radius, thus asphyxiating any and all people who may have managed to find shelter, unless they happen to have oxygen equipment with them.

And the megatonnage says nothing at all about radioactive fallout, the effect feared most of all, the subject of varying calculations and assumptions surrounded by the shibboleths of secretiveness. The direct, immediately lethal radiation is the twin brother of the firestorm, concentrated in the area of detonation. What is most fatal is the rain of radioactive particles that continues after a detonation, carried around the globe by the winds. They are the instruments of slow killing, a showerbath of death falling steadily for days, years, and decades within a global gas chamber. They enter the grass that the cattle eat in the pastures, and they accompany vegetables, meat, and milk into the blood and bones, and the testicles and ovaries, of human beings. They can have an effect, more or less slow, not only on people living today but also on those deep in generations as yet unborn.

One teaspoonful of strontium 90 would be enough, it is said, to kill the entire human race. When a superbomb explodes, whole vats of strontium are thrust into the atmosphere. Only a small portion reaches human beings. Even now, all of us, it appears, are carrying a minute dosage from the nuclear tests, so minute as to be harmless in most cases. But even now, according to reports every year from Hiroshima, victims of the first atom bomb are dying. And scientists have calculated how many children will be born dead or deformed within the next few generations because of the peacetime nuclear tests. There are other scientists who dispute these estimates, and admittedly nothing can be proved one way or the other. But the old theory of a "threshold" of radiation, up to which one may go with impunity ,has no responsible defenders today. The desirable threshold of radioactive radiation for man is no radiation at all.

Every individual carries a set of about a hundred thousand genes—an inheritance he has received from all the living beings who preceded him and concentrated their qualities in him. That is the heritage he will pass on. If all the genes from the world's three and a half billion people were baked together, they would form a small ball with a diameter of about one millimeter. The contents of this small ball is what holds us together as a species, and is, essentially, all we own as human beings. And it is this "property" of ours, the human heritage as such, that is threatened by the radioactive showerbath.

So far no "clean" bomb has been built. A nuclear world war, in any case, would mean a threat of global poisoning. In their arsenals the superpowers possess a destructive force enabling them to annihilate each other many times over— what is called, in the grotesque jargon of the weaponeers, the "overkill" capacity. But the radioactive isotopes know of no concepts such as enemies, allies, or neutrals. Isotopes affect everyone with cosmic impartiality.

Someone, still in the jargon of today, invented the designation "beach" for the amount of nuclear energy that, detonated in the atmosphere, would create enough radioactive fallout to kill half the population of the world—an idea borrowed from the end-of-the-world vision in Nevil Shute's novel, *On the Beach*. The force stored in the nuclear weapons so far produced has been presumed to amount to two or three beach.

Two or three—it is quite enough to qualify as a real threat of annihilation.

The prattling brook along the hikers' route and the threat of global poisoning—they don't jibe. And yet both are realities.

To concentrate for a while on the reality of the brook. It has long evoked sensations of pleasure and tried to drown out other realities. It prattles its way into pleasant memories.

Mountain brooks, one may reason (and one makes an intense effort to keep this fact in sight)—mountain brooks are the friends and companions of the hiker, spelling each other as he proceeds. Sometimes one just hears them trickle and murmur, invisible. Sometimes they are suddenly at one's side with sun and cascading water.

A brook is an invitation to rest. Thinking back to the breaks in past hikes, there is almost always a brook in the picture, and one is tempted by its sociability, now snorting, now confidentially whispering. As one sits there, wiping the sweat from one's forehead and stretching in a feeling of physical well-being, Linnaeus turns up again, this time with something to say about "the precious pearling and delicious water" that "depends on the snow." It is a pleasure to confirm this by lying prone across a rock and letting the chilly water wash over one's face and fill one's mouth.

Once we have had our fill of the precious fluid that

depends on the snow, it is not long before we stand on the ridge and look out over the greenish-brown delta of Veodal valley, and beyond the valley to a panorama that is overwhelming in its severe beauty. There is Steinbuhö, a miniature Matterhorn. Straight ahead, the Glittertind peak with a light cloud around its crest. Glittertind—what festivity in the name. Tomorrow, over the peak. That is our plan.

Almost in despair one asks oneself: are there no safety devices capable of securing the beauty of this world for man—and man for the beautiful world? No safeguards against the threat of erasure?

The "balance of retaliation"? It is based on the awareness that a nuclear war would leave no vanquished on whom a harsh peace or a Babylonian Captivity could be imposed—nor any victor. Country X knows that if by a massive attack it reduces country Y to ruins, country Y will still have enough invulnerable rockets with which to respond, and the massive retaliation will be immediate.

The mechanics of this balance of terror have functioned as a safeguard so far. Perhaps they can continue to do so.

And yet the whole philosophy behind the balance of retaliation is full of contradictions and paradoxes. It tries to tell us that hydrogen bombs in two directions neutralize each other. It makes peace depend on the capability of mutual annihilation.

And it bases itself on a number of premises that must *all* prove to be valid. All fingers on the fatal triggers must be directed by cool heads and iron nerves—forever. No misjudgments concerning the intentions of the adversary will ever be made. No local wars will ever develop into general wars by uncontrollable chain reactions. No essential changes will occur in the power balance itself.

In the years when the Cold War was at its frostiest, whole libraries were written about that most barren of all perspectives—the unintentional war, the war unleashed by accident, by technical error, by human mistake. At their desks, the grand strategists of the atomic age, haunted by the paradox that the very perfecting of techniques could make technical imperfections the more fatal, energetically analyzed and catalogued various risks of error. They illustrated how man's technology itself had catapulted him into a stage where it was no longer possible for anyone to control the game completely.

Thus it was pointed out that a limited action, seemingly safe enough, may trigger sequences of unexpected acts ending in disaster. And that the superpowers in a concrete situation may be tempted to stand pat, each starting from the assumption that the other side will yield out of fear of the consequences—but what if that assumption is unfounded? There was talk of the self-executing prophecy: a casual action by one side may be misinterpreted by the other side as aggressive rather than defensive, leading to defensive measures that could be misinterpreted by the first side, in turn, as aggressive—and so on until the point of no return.

It was demonstrated that technology, a product of human intelligence, was about to put human intelligence out of play. A computer may fail; a message from a radar network, sent at lightning speed over enormous distances, may be misunderstood; an aurora, a moon echo, a meteor, or even a mere flight of wild geese may be interpreted as an enemy attack—such things have in fact happened, and on a few occasions aircraft have been sent up against the presumed foe, only to be recalled just in time.

The goal that weaponeers are aiming at is, after all, to strike ever harder, ever faster, ever more accurately. Today it is possible to send rockets with heavy nuclear payloads and presumed accuracy from one continent to another in half an hour. This gives the responsible leader of a nation only a few minutes' grace after a blip on a radar screen is reported.

It allows him no time for consideration and consultation in an acute crisis. If you choose to wait and verify, it may be too late; if you delay pressing the button, some of your own vulnerable launching pads may be destroyed—*if* there is an actual attack. The very semblance of considered decision, according to some of the analysts, has been removed; the actual decision is made by a radar set or a computer. A misinterpreted impulse or a faulty transistor may decide the fate of civilization.

Who could read these catalogues of how a large portion of humanity might be annihilated by mistake, without being seized by a feeling of being in a lunatic asylum? If nothing else, they showed how close to the abyss we had sometimes been while the Cold War was at its bitterest. With the fail-safe systems acquired by the great nuclear powers since then, war as a result of a technical mishap is said to be less probable now. But nothing, it would seem, can be entirely excluded in a critical situation. In any case, the risk of human error at a moment of excited fear and under the pressure of quick decisions can never be eliminated. And the margin for reaction and decision is bound to shrink to zero when satellites take over the role of rockets in hurling nuclear loads against a target. The time schedule may well be compressed to the point where attack and retaliation become practically simultaneous. And that will indeed be the end of the line in the union of technology and the philosophy of retaliation.

It must be in recognition of this that formulas have been desperately sought, in some quarters, for limiting a great war in spite of everything. One school has found that the mutual fear of atomic weapons will make it possible in the future to wage even a great war with conventional weapons only. This presupposes something that is never said and that nobody in authority can afford to let anybody else as much as suspect—that a nation, even a great power, might be prepared to surrender for the sake of survival. This may be possible

—if it is found that the alternative to surrender is annihilation. But as infatuated as the nations are with the idea of retaliation it is hardly probable that a country in a tight spot would refrain from using the stronger weapons in its arsenal.

Still more unrealistic is the belief that an atomic war might be fought using only minor weapons "in a humane manner," to recall the bizarre words of one of the doting fathers of the hydrogen bomb. Of all illusions, that of "the disciplined nuclear war" is surely the worst folly. Once adversaries in conflict have started throwing Hiroshima-size bombs at each other, it is hard to see them refraining from the use of their larger weapons.

Yet another school, domiciled in the West, has sought a formula for limiting not the weapons but their targets. It has been calculated, with the aid of the Pentagon computers, that a massive surprise attack would immediately annihilate one hundred and fifty million of the one hundred and ninety-five million inhabitants of the United States. But it should be possible to save one hundred million lives, members of this school have assured us, if only both parties proclaim their intention to attack only military targets on the other side, not its cities. Each side could calculate in advance what losses it would suffer in such a no–city war and, in the event of actual war, would electronically compare actual losses with the previously calculated "permissible" ones in order to decide on an appropriate level of retaliation; if the computers showed higher figures, invulnerable weapons of great destructive force would be held back. But the other side has not shown any willingness to play this game. And if it did, what would such a war actually be like? If in the course of a few hours both sides had laid waste each others' vulnerable targets, if by chance the reactions had been simultaneous and the rockets of each side hit launching silos already emptied, while some tens of millions of people had been killed—would they then call the whole thing off?

No guarantees against total holocaust once a great war erupts have been found, and they will almost certainly never be found. No matter from what angle the balance of retaliation is studied, one finds that the more the powers strive to increase their security, the more insecurity they create. The mightier a nation is in means of deterrence, the more exposed to devastation it becomes.

The balance of retaliation! Every hour of every day and night—at this very moment, beyond the stillness of the mountains—there are planes on the wing and submarines on the prowl, loaded with weapons and ready to strike. Rockets with their poisonous charge are hanging ready to be fired on ramps and in silos, their nosecones mathematically aimed at their targets, and not only military targets but also civilian ones—the desk where Bill is working and eating, the bed where Ivan is sleeping or making love. Aimed, perhaps, at my home.

And yet, haven't the nations, joined precisely by their mutual terror, been forced to collect at least some of their wits? After all, a hundred countries have signed an agreement not to poison the atmosphere, outer space, or the oceans by further nuclear tests. The United Nations has solemnly banned nuclear warheads from all space vehicles. A "hot line" has been installed between the White House and the Kremlin. The nuclear powers have announced that they have reduced the production of fissionable material for military purposes. A treaty on nondissemination of nuclear weapons has been ratified by a number of states. The Cold War is no longer quite so frosty as it was.

This can be interpreted as a sign of restraint and responsibility. But we would be lulling ourselves into a false sense of security if we let any thaw-of-the-moment fool us into thinking that we have passed a real turning point .The calm itself may be ominous, blunting our awareness of the dangers to which we are exposed and of the need to get to the root of the evil. The very feeling of a relative absence of danger is itself dangerous, since it may tempt some nations to increased intransigence in mutual conflicts and thus create local combustions into which the great powers may be sucked against their will. The greatest threat, however, is not from the rockets aimed at their assigned targets and ready to be fired today. The greatest threat arises from what is as yet imperfect and incomplete.

For the world is not static. The present balance of power —to the limited extent that there is such a balance—can only be temporary. It is subject to change, and it will most certainly be changed by new technical inventions and by political shuffles.

So far no start has been made toward a real reduction of armaments. At Geneva, that urgent forum of contact, the discussions continue around the green baize table without a single sword having yet been beaten into a plowshare. The disarmament negotiations have not restrained one part from planning for a system of new defensive missiles and the other part from subsequently debating a responding system; nor have they deterred an unrepresented big country from hydrogen bomb tests and development of its own missile system. And while the voices of the negotiators grow hoarse, white-smocked men in laboratories are experimenting with new and even more effective weapons.

If one sees only that arsenals already brimming are not being replenished as fast as before, one loses sight of what is really happening. The superpowers already possess an overkill capacity that many people find absurd. If one is able to annihilate a potential enemy five times over, increasing the arsenals until one can annihilate him ten or fifteen times over seems to make little sense. But the real dynamism of armaments is not in the enlargement of arsenals with more and more weapons already perfected, but in the development of new weapons and counterweapons.

One of the military philosophers of our age has calculated that there is a revolution in weaponry every five years or so. He notes three such revolutions since World War II, marked principally by the perfecting of the atom bomb first, then the hydrogen bomb, and most recently the long-range ballistic missile. He foresees similar revolutions at frequent intervals in the future.

The crises and tests of the Cold War depended, first and foremost, on the assumption of one side that the other was "ahead" at some point and somehow had to be caught up with. The relative quiet of today is the result of a relative status quo. But the day some power gains a head start, either by a new and deadlier weapon or by an effective counter-weapon to the old ones, the balance is suddenly upset—with alarm, tension, and perhaps renewed hectic testing in its wake.

What new instruments of horror the human brain may invent can hardly be foreseen. Who would have thought of the atomic bomb ten years before Alamogordo? Who could have visualized the blinding glare of the hydrogen bomb ten years before Eniwetok? Who, in the terror of the V-2 bombs at the end of World War II, could have dreamt of rockets crossing the oceans in half an hour?

Men residing outside lunatic asylums have been talking seriously of a "doomsday machine" to be placed at an invulnerable depth in the crust of the earth and attached to a computer programmed to react to intolerable acts on the part of other states: if any state violated the code, the computer, without any human brain or human hand being engaged, would electronically release the doomsday machine, and the whole world of man would be blown to bits and pieces. The perfect weapon of retaliation—but more than a trifle annoying if the bang came as a result of some malfunction of a gadget in the electronic system. Other men, equally serious, have suggested bases sunk into the far side of the moon, from which any point on the surface of the earth could be reached by rockets under remote control: thus the earth would be dominated from the moon.

Such ideas may be dismissed as desperate brainstorms in the shadow of the balance of retaliation. Within a decade or so, both the doomsday machine and the moon base may be technically feasible. Today, it is hard to regard them as probable. But that such ideas have even been aired in earnest by supposedly sane men is undeniably a somber sign of our times.

The cool brains of technology have enough to keep them occupied, even without such excursions. Only the purest innocence can believe that the satellites now circling the globe have been launched out of sheer and uncorrupted intellectual curiosity; the enormous sums they devour would never have been put up if the exploration of space had not been thought to be of military importance. The world of the future may be shaped by what such satellites carry in their noses. Even today it would probably be possibly to blanket a nation with rockets carrying nuclear warheads, stationary carriers of death from our earthbound viewpoint, which would rotate with the earth and could be released from a remote command center or by direct fire—a veritable sword of Damocles in the nuclear age.

Or maybe the next step will be the development of counterweapons. So far the technique of a rocket war has been that of scatter-gunning a large number of rockets against a target; only a few will have nuclear warheads, the rest are dummies, and there has been no way of pinpointing the dangerous projectiles in this rain of bombs. Even now, colossal sums of money are being spent on developing the laser—the death ray—an enormous concentration of energy capable of cutting through a yard of armor as easily as a knife through butter, and of traveling at the speed of light to destroy, in a fraction of a second, atom and hydrogen bombs in flight. The idea is to have a chain of manned space stations from which all rocket launchings could be checked and the rockets destroyed in midair with the aid of the "light gun." The first state to neutralize nuclear weapons in this manner would gain an enormous political supremacy.

The present warning and weapons systems may perhaps also be put out of business by dislocating their electronic instruments or disrupting magnetic fields.

But all this speculation only applies to the things we know today. Our imagination is not powerful enough to give us any real idea of what the next few decades may produce if the arms race continues. Premonition itself stands mute. We can be sure of only one thing: weapons will breed counter-weapons and the new counter-weapons newer weapons in turn, all giving rise to constant changes in the balance and to new crises.

Even so, we might perhaps dare believe that the present situation could have room for some kind of atom-age counter-part to Pax Romana or The Holy Alliance, if only the map of political power remained stable. But this is not the case. We may have been indulging in too much sterile thinking in terms of East and West, thus failing to understand that we are living in a world of change. While relations between the present superpowers, rich and conservative as they both are, have reached a measure of stability and even community of interest, the emergence of new power factors may lead to even more severe political convulsions than those we witnessed before the present power blocs attained mutual balance.

Then, if not before, the philosophy behind the balance of retaliation will surely fail. If not even the small first steps have been taken toward real disarmament, in the long run no new international treaties will be able to prevent an ever-increasing number of states from acquiring nuclear weapons. And a generation that experienced the corporal and his war can hardly feel confident that all nations, in all situations, will be guided by reason. Who is to guarantee that the combatants in some local conflict, one that means life and death for them, will refrain from recourse to the strongest weapons available? Who dares to imagine that a state with frontiers bulging with overpopulation and having nothing to lose will have the same fear of pressing the trigger as that of today's rich superpowers? And once a nuclear war has erupted, there is inevitably the risk that it will soon swell until it embraces the entire balloon of the earth.

But suppose that the safeguards work, that the explosion can be avoided for another few decades while societies are increasingly militarized through and through, while the Ragnarok machinery is incessantly perfected and the world hurled from crisis to crisis? What will be the human condition in such a world?

Even the generation that has passed the epochal line can visualize only vaguely the psychological effects of living under the constant threat of annihilation—an existence in which the whole social machinery must inevitably become robotized, in which individuals are forced to flee from one defense device to another, each more humiliating than the one before, in which the constant threat of radioactive pollution may make the Geiger counter and the dosimeter—for measuring the radioactivity around us and the doses we ourselves absorb—accessories as commonplace as the fountain pen and the wristwatch.

What must be considered probable is that freedom and democracy, in the senses we have hitherto known, are going to be in a tight spot. In a world under permanent threat, permanent fear, permanent preparedness with the finger on the trigger, in such a world things like finesse and forbearance, consideration and tolerance, must become not merely risky extravagances but dangerous weaknesses. The deeper values of social co-existence, the very things that the weapons were to protect, may be crushed to pulp by them without their having actually been fired even once. There will be continued existence but little or no meaningful life.

Yet all of this could mean no more than a temporary extension of existence, a delay in the eruption. The world of the future will probably harbor no illusions about arming itself away from war by continuing to improve the efficiency of its instruments of destruction. In this, surely, lies the deepest debasement: a humanity that believes in the inevitability of war and can do no better than to try to extend its existence from day to day because the horrors of war appear perhaps a few degrees worse than those of peace. But then somebody, or perhaps a few, may even come to believe that waiting in the shadow of disaster is less bearable than the disaster itself—that since the big bang will be heard someday no matter what we do, one might just as well have the whole thing over with immediately. And then? . . .

Perhaps collective suicide will be consummated. Perhaps our drama will have a Grand Finale in which all history ends, in which the very memory of man, of his development, and of his struggle, is obliterated. Only a few man-made moons will still circle the Martian landscape that had been the residence of life, to tell of the possibilities man had possessed and squandered. Space hears nothing, sees nothing. in its cold, unremembering infinity it will be as if we had never existed in our marginal home.

Or perhaps the annihilation will not be complete. Perhaps a small vestige of the human race will be rescued, protected by the cave existence of a new age. Rescued for what?

Life in the shelters of nuclear war, sunk under the surface of the earth or deep within the cloak of the polar icecap, must mean almost unbearable travail. Those shreds of humanity who have escaped the whirlwind and who, buried alive for weeks and months, can only wait for the radioactivity above their heads to spend itself, must know that they have experienced, are experiencing, the greatest catastrophe ever suffered by the home of man. What kind of life awaits them on the day they crawl out of their caves?

What this shred of humanity encounters on that day is bound to be a silent and unknown world. No Noah's ark will have saved any of man's companion creatures from the flood of radioactivity. The mammals will have been swept away; their poisoned carcasses lie rotting in the fields and woods. The song of birds will have ended. No bluethroat plays its silver chimes, no flock of wild geese draws its plow against a blue sky. Instead, clouds of insects and colonies of bacteria are lying in wait. While a dose of six hundred röntgen is deadly for human beings, insects are not harmed by dosages even several hundred times that. They are the creatures who will possess the earth once the radioactive isotopes have done their work. With the delicate balance of nature abolished, with no birds to keep them in check, they must have multiplied incalculably.

In this new world the few survivors of the human species will have to start the elementary hunt for food without delay. Meat and milk are no longer available, except in dispersed hoards of cans that may have escaped destruction. The plants of the soil are all poisoned in varying degrees. There is bound to be a primitive, wild, and cruel struggle for existence among various plundering flocks. The whole fine texture of relationships in human society, the whole complicated machinery of coexistence, will have been blown to pieces. The only survivors of a species that raised a Buddha, a Socrates, a Christ, that pondered the riddles of the stars and even found the key to the structure of creation, will be a few shocked, starving, disease-ridden hordes of barbarians, without any firm anchorage in the past, without hope for the future.

Will the survivors envy the dead?, Herman Kahn wonders

in his musings on the unthinkable. Never has a question been posed that is more frightening—and more humiliating—for humanity.

The slowly trickling radioactive showerbath will continue, through years and decades. Some will have survived the cave existence of the shelters only to meet death by poisoning. Others will go on living and go on conceiving with a ruined mass of genes that may produce a race quite different from the one that once, in exaggerated self-esteem and without a sense of the grim irony, designated itself as Homo sapiens, "wise man."

Is this the destiny—the global community grave or the dehumanized existence in a poisoned world—towards which they are all marching—all these black, yellow, brown, and white soldiers whose robotlike footsteps echo in the silence of the mountains? Is this where we are all drifting blindly, on a course we lack the wisdom or courage to change?

I look at my companion walking ahead of me so securely and confidently, and I shiver in the evening sun. I know why I cannot escape what is going on beyond the ridges. It concerns me, for it affects him, my companion.

At dusk smoke-gray clouds are drifting through the valley. There will be rain tomorrow. I can see it in the clouds and feel it in the wind sliding down from the mountains in the west.

2

*". . . within us lives the
ever-present past . . ."*

THE RAIN COMES IN HEAVY BURSTS THROUGH VEODAL
valley, carried by a brisk gale. There is no point in trying Glittertind peak today, and we decide to cross Skautflyi.

Even down here the wind is so strong that we have to
butt our way ahead. Sometimes, in the strongest gusts, we
have to stop for a moment and dig in our heels before we
can go on. The rain is almost horizontal. It smites our faces
with wet gloves.

This is not exactly the kind of day we would have wished
for, but we shout to each other something about the beauty
of the rain and how refreshing it is, and what an advantage
not to have to walk through the desert with burning palate
and swollen tongue looking for water holes. And the wind *is*
good, cleansing and clear; there is a fine tone in its horn.

We actually enjoy ourselves.

To our left, the Veo glacier sticks out a grayish-white
tongue, seeming to relish the rain, licking it up.

We stop for a moment to look at the glacier. One can

30

sense it, any glacier, as a living creature, constantly on the move, slowly but persistently at work. A glacier feeds on snow at the top, melting it into tough, wandering ice that ranges in hue between emerald and cobalt in the melting zones and is now porous like a lung, now as firm and clear as crystal. It digs and burrows in the mountain, chews, grinds, kneads, and at the glacier gate it leaves walls and half-ringed mountains of silt and a porridge of rocks and sometimes whole boulders, and rills and rivulets starting their journey towards the sea, a little uncertainly, carrying some of the silt along for company. Standing by a glacier you can hear the roar of water at its melting work inside. The giant is gargling in his mountain home.

Glaciers yield a vision of the life of a mountain. For mountains are not immutable sentries, standing since the dawn of time, standing fast as millions of years roll by and species emerge and disappear. If you look for immutability, you find no more of it in the mountains than elsewhere.

What I cannot see but can sense, somehow, is the violent interior life of the mountains, the microcosmic events—the dance of the electrons around their nucleus in the minature universe of each atom and the constant little atomic explosions that slowly transform parts of the interior of mountains. But I can read, fragmentarily, the exterior record of evolution, and I find such fragments when my companion and I resume our hike, fighting our way towards the ridge between the peaks of Veotind and Ryggehö.

I can walk here and pretend to remember—for in some way I was present—how enormous quantities of silt, washed down through the ages from the surface of the earth, built up enough pressure to break through the bottom crust of the Silurian sea hundreds of millions of years ago. How the magma rose, masses of sediment were compressed, and a mountain chain emerged from the depths and raised nameless peaks over a world where the first fish were testing out their talent for swimming in the oceans and where ferns were wandering over the land. How erosion and levelling began almost immediately, with the obliging assistance of heavy rains, so that the mountains were largely eroded into a plateau by the time the convulsions of the earth's crust, in the tertiary period, hurled their swell up here and lifted the roof again.

Since then erosion has again done its yeoman work diligently. Running water has dug furrows in the slopes and widened some furrows into valleys. Glaciers have gnawed and cut down large parts of the mountains and left souvenirs in the form of these dark mountain lakes, which seem to rest within themselves. The shapes of the mountains were formed around the tough and heavy kinds of rock that withstood the chisels of time better than others.

As one roams through mountain country, it is generally quite easy to distinguish the riper shapes, kneaded in earlier eras, from the handiwork of more recent geological architecture: pointed peaks, often with sheer walls. But here, too, erosion goes its unstoppable way. Rain and melting water seep into crevices, ice loosens boulders that roll down and collect in a growing ring around the feet of the peaks, water grinds and files away. Some glaciers have not come to rest even now. I know precious little about tomorrow's weather, but I do know that at some future time—in another few hundred million years—this whole mountain massif will have been ground down, its peaks cut off, and what was once the craggy home of the giants will be a plain with only slight, rolling elevations.

The rain has increased—a fugue of hissing sounds and at the same time, by a small portion, the abrasive that over millions of years tirelessly files down these mountain cathedrals, which for a puny human second inspire solemnity and awe.

We can read the history of the mountains, at least some

of it. And we can foresee their future. But what do we really know about our own species, which was formed from the dust of the earth just as the mountains were? What evolution brought Homo sapiens to the point where we stand today, in the shadow of the cosmic poison mushroom?

In the myths of man from disparate cultures there are recurrent images of some lost golden age. There is the Garden of Eden before the snake had yet tempted man with the forbidden fruits of knowledge. There is the godlike golden race first imagined by the masters of the Olympus, then replaced by a less godlike silver race, succeeded by a bronze race, and followed in turn by the imperfect iron race to which we belong.

Latter-day social reformers in the West based themselves on similar concepts. Rousseau built his system on the illusion of the original good. His "retournons à la nature," consistently caricatured in the sham rococo pastorales of the eighteenth century, promised secular salvation if only man would return to rosy-cheeked, bucolic innocence. The social utopians followed much the same line. Thus Robert Owen felt that he could predict "with mathematical certainty" that under satisfactory social conditions man would be happy and good—again. Even Karl Marx banked heavily on the illusion of man's original goodness and peacefulness when, in a spirit of secular messianism, he conceived the vision of a re-denationalized human community in which there would be neither exploiters nor exploited.

The truly revolutionary contribution of Charles Darwin was that he pulled aside a veil from the prehistory of the human race and showed us a merciless world in which all living things were engaged in a universal struggle for survival and only the best equipped had a chance of staying alive for long. This was the murder of Santa Claus, and it did away with the belief in a paradise lost. Granted that Darwin managed to merge his subversive visions with the prevalent evolutionary optimism of his day and felt that he could confidently foresee a development towards ever greater progress and perfection. Granted also that the room for doubt left in his cautious seeking received little notice from his first evolution-happy interpreters. Yet nobody has done more than the solitary thinker on the Down to help us advance toward the "know thyself" that was the heart of Socrates' wisdom.

If we want to understand the dark forces within ourselves, surely we must give up the haughty idea that we are unique in all creation. We are parts of a whole, and the behavior of the other species of life within that whole can teach us something about ourselves. Several latter-day followers of Darwin who have pursued such a track have been able to demonstrate that a "territorial instinct" is one of the strongest motivating forces in the struggle for survival. It is too fundamental for its ancient origins to be traced, but everywhere—among reptiles and fish, birds and mammals—a passionate urge to possess a territory of one's own, along with an aggressive posture in defense of it, is to be seen. It is an outflow of the primary instinct to find the food that is needed to sustain life. Possession of one's own territory guarantees food and thus increases the chance of survival.

Roaring tigers and lions patrol the territory they have conquered by virtue of their strength and protect it against intruders of their own species. The song of birds is rarely a sentimental hymn to the joy of life and idyllic peace; it starts when the male has claimed a territory, and its practical aim is to proclaim to other birds of the same species that he has found his living space and is ready to fight for it. Place a couple of aquariums side by side, each with a male fighting-fish in it. If an opaque screen is interposed between the aquariums the fish swim about without a care in the world, but if the screen is removed they rush at each other, menacingly flexing gills and fins through the glass, until one of them feels defeated and skulks away to the farthest part of his domain.

It is some consolation that some living creatures also have their doctrine of neutrality. Thus flocks of antelope graze on different parts of the savanna but respect the neutrality of the water hole. Seals roar to protect their property, once they have divided the rock and collected their females, but share neutral corridors for passage in and out of the water. Birds find neutral sites for picking seeds and worms outside their own territories—and there the male never sings.

Among man's closest relatives the territorial instinct is very strongly developed. This has been repeatedly shown— as by, for example, the probing naturalist C. R. Carpenter, who made the experiment of moving a number of monkeys from India to a small island of Puerto Rico in order to study their pattern of behavior within the limited space of an island. On board ship, where there was no land to divide, all social ties were dissolved and complete anarchy soon resulted. But within a year after the monkeys had been landed on the island, they had again organized themselves in social groups and divided the island among themselves, with each group living in permanent hostility toward the neighboring flocks.

Baboons—"the people sitting on their heels," as they are called by the Bushmen, almost as if they were colleagues —operate in groups on a constant war footing, guarding their territories militantly. The typical group is one of the largest among any of the primates, probably because it is surrounded on all sides by skulking enemies. It follows a leader, apparently has a council of elders, and comprises a number of strong males surrounded by a harem and a few bachelors who were defeated in the sex battle but are valuable to the group for their contributions to defense and pillage.

When the aborigines of Australia, Tierra del Fuego, and the Amazon delta were "discovered," they were found to be living in tribes of almost the same size as the social groups of the baboons. With a certain justification they have been spoken of as "living fossils."

The study of other species and their behavior has been enough to allow a ray of light to fall on the branch of the primates that eventually gave rise to man, but the last few decades have brought us new etching fluids that should help to develop the picture even more clearly. The skulls of beings of a million years ago and their tools in the struggle for existence, which were found at the edge of the Kalahari desert by Raymond Dart (a scholar long underestimated), have revealed more about the prehistory of man than anything else discovered since Darwin's day. The excavations of the Leakeys in the region around Lake Victoria have yielded supplementary evidence. The various parts fit together like pieces in a jigsaw puzzle. We begin to be able to see something of ourselves in the mirror of time.

At some moment about twenty million years ago—this is how the picture is beginning to emerge before our eyes—a group of tree-climbing primates broke out of the jungle and embarked on a more adventurous life on the sun-baked savannas of eastern Africa. Unlike the rest of the forest apes, they had developed a taste for meat—perhaps because a change of climate had thinned the forests and reduced the supply of vegetable foods. In any case, the hunger for meat led them to seek larger hunting grounds. The ape that left the shaded existence of the jungle as predatory, a carcass eater, a murderer. Slowly he learned to stand erect to scan the horizon for prey and foes—a necessity in the life of a hunter on open ground.

There, on the windswept high plains between Kenya and the Cape, the overture began in a drama that would lead to the symphonies of Beethoven, the brooding of Hamlet, the dream factories of Hollywood—and Hiroshima.

From the hairy primate who first left the darkness of

the forest, staggering uncertainly on his feet, developed the individual—neither ape nor man, a proto-human with the erect body of man and the narrow cranium of an ape—that Dart found in the limestone caves of the Makapansgat Valley, and the being with an already enlarged brain cavity, that was brought back into daylight by Leakey at the Olduvai Gorge.

In flocks they emerged from the jungle, in flocks they continued hunting on the savanna. In descriptions of the development of human society toward ever increasing complexity it has been customary to say that the family came first, that families banded together into tribes, and that tribes united into nations. Actually, the family was probably preceded by the flock, for the flock meant protection against the many dangers in the struggle for existence. In a flock, larger animals could be attacked, in a flock there was a better chance to defend one's territory against others. The group became a defense for the individual, and therefore the individual defended the group. In this way the group bred a dawning solidarity based on the instinct of self-preservation, which is found even among baboons.

And there, within the group of hunters and seekers after meat, the weapon was invented. At first a stick or a stone, extending the arm and increasing its strength. Then the club. Dart's finds in Makapan and Swartkrans show that a favorite weapon of the low-browed hunters of about a million years ago was the upper foreleg of the ordinary antelope. It became a double club with which it was possible not only to attack larger animals but also to make war on the other flocks of one's own species—and perhaps even the neutrality around water holes, so small and dwindling under the hot African sun, was violated. With the weapon in its hairy fist, the predatory animal had reached some distance beyond itself. The weapon increased the margin of survival. Whether Dart's discovery represents a direct forebear of man or an extinguished sideline, it does constitute evidence that when man finally entered on the stage of evolution, the weapon was already in his hand.

My companion has halted. Something else occupies him. He shows how the snow reaches into a small mountain pond and shines in an intense, bluish white under the surface. What remains of the snow is in evidence at unusually low elevations this year, all the way down to the foot of the mountain in many places; it has been a cool summer. Thus the mountain vegetation remains green, with only a few splashes of rust.

We have been walking for a while on ground-down mountain, hearing water trickling under the rocks. On the left, the tongues of the glacier have followed us: leftovers for the last ice age, like the white icecaps of the poles, and slowly thawing. After all, it is only twelve thousand years since the fourth ice age, with its enormous blanket of ice, began its retreat. Probably we are still only on our way out of it.

The rain has turned into hail but the clouds are lighter and the sun comes out from time to time. Sun and hail and relics of the ice age—we are far from the yellow savannas of Africa.

Or perhaps not so far, after all. Perhaps the ice ages had something to do with the appearance of man on the continent where our drama opened. The million years during which great freezes swept back and forth over the northern hemisphere were the period that saw manlike beings emerge from apelike ones. It was a time of violent changes of climate and much volcanic activity. All this could well have given rise to mutations, which may explain how the brain of the weapon-carrying primate was suddenly tripled in size—suddenly in the course of a few hundreds of thousands of years—after millions of years of very slow development. Evolution worked at piece rates, and other manlike species emerged under the hammer. Some were soon rejected as unfit, others managed to go on. The changing, and sometimes harsh, climate increased the requirements for survival and favored intelligence. The brain took on a definite function in the process of natural selection.

If so, then man was more of an accident than a probability. It was in the nature of evolution to produce increasingly complex forms—but not necessarily man. If a group of primates had not developed a taste for meat, if they had not left the protected life of the forest, if the ice ages had not swept the globe, if this or that mutation had not occurred —it is possible to produce long columns of ifs.

Accident! As an individual, each human being is an accident. Each gift of the male to the female includes hundreds of thousands of cells capable of fertilizing, but only one of them can join the ovum. A different hour for the embrace or a different cell winning the race, and an individual would have been created who would have been like me in many ways but who would not have possessed exactly my combination of genes. Among millions of possibilities there was only one that could lead to "me."

But if the individual is a product of coincidences, should not the same be true of species? Even species man?

And at what bend in the road of evolution did man become man? When did the transition occur from manlike ape to apelike man?

Was it when the realization of an "I" awoke? And when did this happen? The empty skulls of Makapan and Olduvai give no answer.

Or was it when grunts and cries began to be articulated into a language? When sounds, the atoms of thought, began being built into words, the molecules of thought, and these eventually into sentences, the cells of thought? One can sense that this process was connected with the sudden development of the big brain. In any case, language created new possibilities of cohesion within the flock. New opportunities, too, of conveying something of past experience to new generations.

Or was it when the erect creature took fire into its service? It must have been an enormous event when some low-browed individual, alarmed at his own audacity but moved by the curiosity and lust for conquest that has been so characteristic of the human race, dared for the first time to approach a tree split by lightning and to steal the fire. That it was a momentous, a terrifying event is proved by its having been memorialized for so long a time in the various Prometheus myths. Perhaps no other deed in the history of the human race can be considered its equivalent, until we in our generation started to finger the inside of nature in the same curious manner. In any case, whereas lightning suddenly shooting forth from the clouds and sometimes setting trees on fire had long created only fear—the atavistic terror that many people still feel in a thunderstorm—now the flocks could huddle 'round the camp fire, light could be brought into caves that had been dark, raw meat could be cooked. A path to civilization was opening up.

Or did animal become man when its coarse mouth was curved into a smile for the first time?

There is no one point at which we can stop and say "Here is where it happened." Gradually, unnoticed, in the course of some hundreds of thousands of years, man came into being.

But whenever man finally appeared, the weapon was in his fist. And it had been there for a long time.

Perhaps—the shameless suspicion is there—perhaps the weapon was a link in the chain of events that made man into man. The weapon increased the need for precision, for co-ordination of the movement of muscles and thereby the demands on the coordinating mechanism, the brain. First an armed killer with deeply rooted fighting and territorial instincts, then the big brain, then man.

This was not the picture Rousseau had in mind when he preached a return to nature. For him the leaf-covered slopes of the Jura mountains loomed, not the yellow savannas of Africa.

But without this Cain with the antelope club in his hairy fist, we would not be here. Jesus and Judas, Plato and Herostratos, Buddha and Jenghiz Khan, Einstein and Hitler—they have all sprung from his loins.

We are not unique, but the weapon and the big brain became our characteristics and gave us supremacy over the other species. We became the most successful predatory animals in creation. And the most bloodthirsty.

Of the various possibilities for man that emerged from the laboratory of evolution, only one, Homo sapiens, has survived. The flat-headed pithecantropine human being, who was once spread over the entire Old World from Algeria to China, disappeared. The Neanderthal race, having ruled for a hundred thousand years between the two latest ice ages, went the same way. Was it broken by a hardening climate, or did our race, handier with weapons and more skilled in killing, wipe it out? The earth provides no answer.

But we are able to see that from our very beginnings, with the help of our weapons and tools, we have overbearingly interfered with natural selection. Species emerge and disappear naturally, but we have hastened the disappearance of many a species long before the forces of nature were finished with it. Beings shaped by millions of years of creative power have been annihilated, or at least decimated to the point of near annihilation, in an astonishingly short time. No tallyho will ever be sounded to greet the shooting of a dodo bird. The whale, the mightiest mammal on earth, which left its existence on dry land to let its final shape be streamlined by the oceans, seems about to go the way of the mammoth. Forests and jungles are being forced back, leaving less and less living space for the creatures waging their existence in them. The gorilla and the orangutan, beings belonging to the same family as ourselves, are moving in the twilight of species.

And not least, weapon-bearing man has become his own mortal enemy. He need not fear the beasts of the forests, only himself.

No more than a hundredth of the living beings of creation have been predatory animals. Most wild beasts feed on other animals but avoid their own species. But man, until recent times, has eaten man—and with relish. The split skulls from the caved-in limestone grottoes of China tell a disquieting story about the diet of Peking man just a quarter of a million years ago. Even Cro Magnon man, the mammoth hunter and cave artist who appeared fifty thousand years ago in the forests from which Neanderthal man had disappeared, the tall man with a brain an eighth larger than our own, a man so fully equipped physically and mentally that it would be presumptuous to suppose that the species had improved in any way since his day—Cro Magnon man was a habitual cannibal. Vestiges of his habits are still alive in us.

Blood deliberately shed had a central place in the first groping cults of man, and from Cro Magnon times to the present the sacrifice has continued. Pungent smoke rose from hecatombs of animals sacrificed on altars outside Troy and Carthage, in the Sinai desert, and in the groves of the Norse gods. The greatest sacrifice was man himself, man sacrificed to placate or thank the gods—even the "son of God" sacrificed to redeem the human race. The Aztec priests lifting a still-quivering human heart towards the sun god from the top of their soaring temples are not very far removed from us. On any Sunday in the churches of the western world, the blood of the son of God, shed for thee, and his body, given for thee, are symbolically drunk and eaten. And there is some of the old sacrificial mystery in the excitement at a bullfighting arena or a boxing ring.

But above all else, man has used his weapons in constant enmity towards other groups of his own species. Flocks multiplied into tribes, tribes into nations, nations into alliances. The sounds of language were combined into words such as "nationalism"—at exalted moments, "patriotism" and "love of country"—all of them nothing but paraphrases of the primordial territorial instinct that was woven into our behavior pattern by natural selection.

The big brain, the gift of the ice ages to a meat-hunting primate, was used by man to perfect his weapons. The arm seeking its prey was extended further: from the club to the spear and the bow. Eventually, its strength was increased many times over on the day when cannon began their thunder, never since stilled. And then one day it found its strength increased a trillion times in the hydrogen bomb. From the antelope club capable of splitting a skull to the weapon that could sterilize the entire globe—the releasing forces in the background remained the same.

To his gods man gave the task of helping him overwhelm others of his species. The god whom a wandering pastoral people hunting for new territory had brought with them became a Lord-of-the-Armies who would help destroy those who had taken previous possession of the promised land. A blast of his nostrils gathered together the waters, and by the greatness of his arm other people were as still as stone. "I will send my fear before thee . . . and I will make all thine enemies turn their backs unto thee."

War became as one with the history of man. Ever since the Egyptians and Sumerians began carving their historical accounts, stories of butchery and battles have been committed to clay or bronze. Into our own generation the billowing battle has continued, differing only by its becoming ever the more merciless and all-encompassing. From the bloody encounters of flocks and tribes to the world wars—always the same naked struggle for territory, even though sometimes thinly masked in some religious doctrine or political ideology. In sum, the history of man can be read as the story of a species more wantonly aggressive and self-destructive than any other in creation.

Somewhere, in certain limestone caves south of the moon, a few empty skulls are grinning, as if to say, "We are behind you, we will always be with you."

In front of two lonely mountain hikers a rainbow is rising, painting the slopes of Godhö and Skauthö a hazy bluish red. It seems to be only a few hundred yards in front of us. We have the feeling that at any moment we may enter through it. But it recedes, keeping its distance.

I grope for something else, also receding, just as evasive. I try to capture it in concepts—urges, instincts, dormant reminiscences, ambitions—but any such designation becomes an oversimplification. Within us lives the ever-present past, made up of forces for which we have no names.

All we really know is that these forces must exist. The body of man is the product of a long evolution, and it cannot be different with his nature. Just as the fetus in nine brief months in the womb repeats the whole enormous process of evolution over five hundred million years, so the original brain must preserve nameless forces, experiences, and patterns of reaction from everything that came before. The present, in my psyche as much as in my body, is a vessel containing the entire past. Nothing inherited from the host of living creatures out of whom I emerged can be permanently destroyed. Much may be hidden, suppressed, sublimated—but nothing is erased completely.

Vilhelm Ekelund, the Swedish writer, once spoke of the

past that hides deep down, a strange town, Vineta, in ruins at the bottom of the sea: "You must become like the ocean in a day of September stillness, if you are to hear the chimes of its bells, see the figures wandering in the transparent deep; look all the way into the clear bottom of everything human. There—inside yourself—is *history*."

What Ekelund saw in the transparent deep was Nazareth and Hellas. But the history within us goes far deeper, and the transparent deep is blurred, the more so, the deeper we go. We cannot see the bottom, but somewhere there in the dark moves a being with a low forehead and drooping eyebrows, his club lifted to strike. I am carrying his genes, and so are all my fellow wanderers of species man.

What do I know about him? Essentially, no more than what the caves in the Makapan valley have told us: his urge to kill—an urge that became a necessity for him in the battle for existence.

If the picture we see of ourselves in the mirror of time seems ugly, that is a matter of complete indifference. We cannot change it. That paradise of innocence, that golden age of perfection to which we might wish to return—it never existed. Our Vineta is the wilderness. We carry it within us, and we cannot free ourselves by denying its reality.

Perhaps we simply have to become better acquainted with it. Perhaps there is some chance of mastering the wilderness if we recognize its existence openly and without shame, if we familiarize ourselves with the dark inherited impulses within us—impulses that may explain the mutual distrust of groups and nations and our inclination to rely on weapons and terror for security.

This is how Dart himself interprets the message of the grinning skulls: we have tried many doctrines of redemption—religious, philosophical, political—but it is time, now, to try building on the truth about ourselves.

Without yielding to the lure of earlier illusions, it should be possible to believe that the evidence of the caves is not complete, that it has given the "truth" only piecemeal. Woven into the behavior pattern of the creature down there in the blur were instincts that now threaten to destroy the entire species. This is what we can see and what we are forced to see. But there must also have been something else—burgeoning, imperfect, but springing from the same source. The ever-vigilant distrust of other groups, the *en garde* position, the killing in the hunt for food and in attack and defense, all this was an outflow of the urge for self-preservation—a strong outflow that was to supply the dark woof in the history of man. But out of the urge for self-preservation there must also have sprung loyalty towards the group, which gave rise to budding feelings of tenderness, consideration, and guilt. The loyalty of the small flock was widened to include the tribe, the nation, the alliance. Like a torch lighting the darkness of the cave, it sometimes yielded flickering ideas of universal brotherhood in the minds of a few exceptional beings apart; they never managed to make themselves heard above the roar and clang of weapons, but they did bear the message that the cruelty of the human animal was not necessarily total and unconditional. From the savannas of the low-browed club wielder came not only Jenghiz Khan but also Ichnaton and Socrates, Christ and Buddha.

Here and there, in isolated spots on the planet, peaceful, unarmed human societies have come into being. Eventually they have been crushed by armed might, but the fact that they ever existed is not unimportant.

Man cannot change his nature. But he *is* composed of various possibilities. Perhaps if he became familiar enough with the dark forces at the bottom of the pit, his chances of influencing the screening and direction of these possibilities might improve.

Today, then, man's naked urge for self-preservation

ought to give rise to some new pattern of behavior, for man is now faced with a situation unparalleled in the long history of evolution. Our peering into the interior of nature has pushed us into a new dimension, one in which patterns that were formed ages ago out of the urge for self-preservation can only lead to utter self-destruction.

In earlier wars, aggressions could be unleashed against a visible enemy; not so in the clinically impersonal war envisaged for the future, in which a human automaton, perhaps directed by a computer, presses a button to annihilate people on the other side of an ocean. Earlier wars, including the corporal's, were a more or less naked struggle for living space and territories; in a nuclear war there is no territory to conquer nor any to defend, since the attacked and the attackers are alike threatened with annihilation. In earlier wars the man at the front was presumed to be sacrificing himself out of loyalty to his group and in the belief that he had a reasonable chance to defend his family and his nation; in a war of hydrogen bombs everything he was supposed to defend would perish with him.

Some meaning, whatever it was, could be imputed to earlier wars. The hydrogen bomb has made the waging of war an exercise in global futility.

The dilemma cannot be resolved by cries for a ban on the bomb. Scrap all the bombs and all the rockets, tear down the nuclear plants, and the bomb will still be around, potentially. Knowledge of it cannot be erased. In another great war, which from the outset would certainly be fought with a brutality never seen before, it would not be long before the factories were rebuilt and hydrogen bombs began to plant their poisonous mushrooms.

And the capacity of the human brain to conceive ever more efficient weapons does not stop even with the hydrogen bomb. There has been comparatively little talk about the possibilities of bacteriological warfare, yet sizable stores

47

of poisons and bacteria exist that even in small doses could destroy all living things. The bacterial weapon is admirably inexpensive—"the poor man's H-bomb"—and an attack can be mounted by stealth: a ship approaching the coast of a country in the dark of night can spray it with bacteria, starting an epidemic whose origin would remain a mystery. Certain of the more infamous devices can be risky for the attacker too, and this might act as a deterrent to their use unless the attacker immunized himself in advance. Another possibility, equally close, may well be meteorological warfare—war by climate control. Thus, there has been serious talk of manipulating the weather so as to afflict another country with a devastating drought, or perhaps a new ice age.

Truly, once we feel at liberty to monkey with the forces of nature, the possibilities for doing mischief are innumerable.

There is, then, only one road away from the abyss: to abolish war as an institution. Of course, such an act would be something unique in the bloodstained history of mankind. But then our whole situation is unique.

In the past we have managed to rid ourselves of cruelties that were once regarded as part of the very order of nature. Human beings are no longer sacrificed—in the physical sense —to placate the gods. The last century saw the abolition, by and large, of slavery and the traffic in human beings. In some ways, at least, we have been able to modify deeply ingrained patterns of behavior. Admittedly, the abolition of war as an institution would be a much more difficult, far-reaching task, and one may well be seized with a gnawing doubt of our ability to accomplish it, nailed down as we are in ancient patterns of thought and action. Yet this is the only direction for the urge of self-preservation to point in this day and age. Our whole predicament is this: ancient urges must be guided into new channels in order that our marginal home in space can remain, if only for a few more cosmic seconds, a domicile for creatures of intelligence—for man, the marginal being.

The rain has ended in a whimper. In Visdal valley the wind thunders ahead with renewed vigor. But the clouds have been torn apart and show blue windows.

Ahead of us is Svellnosi, embraced by the century-old ice of Stygge and Svellnos glaciers. We catch a glimpse, now and then, of the peak of Galthöpiggen.

And somewhere down from the willow lands the shrill cry of the mountain finch reaches us. He tells the others of his kind: "Here is my living space; don't come near, or I strike!"

3

NIGHT ON THE MOUNTAIN. HARDLY MORE THAN A sheer, opal twilight. All around are the smoky-gray outlines of the mountains.

The wind has swept the sky clean of the last clouds and come to rest. The lanterns of space are very bright, shining with the brightness of August.

You never see the stars so clearly as from the mountains or on the open sea. And never does the Milky Way sparkle so magnificently in our latitudes as it does in late summer and early fall, when the season of white nights is over and before the stars have taken on their winter pallor.

Mountain and stars—and a quiet so complete that the present appears to lose its reality.

In spite of their bewildering distances away from us, the stars seem to come close on a night like this. And yet it is a paradox of our time that we have come as far away from the stars as we have. In just a few decades, astronomy has taught us more about the nature of the stars than was learned by all previous generations of men, but as the old myths have been abandoned, the stars have ceased to play any real role in our everyday existence. This is probably why we have not really succeeded in merging them with the new conception of the world that must follow from our probing into the cosmos.

Simpler cultures were closer to the stars. Primitive man, with his superstitious view of nature, often felt a direct link between himself and the heavenly lights. They lived in his myths, they promised good hunting or a good harvest, they stood over him during his nocturnal embraces and in his battles with others of his kind. When he ventured outside his own territory, they guided his steps toward known or unknown goals. His star-gazers knew more about the position of the celestial bodies than do most of today's specialized scholars outside the circle of the astronomers.

An episode told by the Norwegian traveler Jens Bjerre comes to mind. In his book about the Kalahari desert, he recalled spending a certain night under the stars among the bushmen, this poor remnant of Africa's aborigines, who have been forced back to the arid rim of the desert. Suddenly the chief pointed with great excitement to a brilliant star, new in his sky. It was not until a week later that what had happened became clear to the white observer: the first sputnik had risen in the firmament.

How very little remains of the star-spangled sky when you see it as a strip from the canyon of a city street! Who then combs the hair of Berenice, who puts the imaginary horses in front of the Wain of Charles?

It is easy to understand how it was that in most cultures star-gazing was the beginning of the physical sciences. How fascinating it must have been for the human intellect, how gratifying, to succeed in establishing the regularity of celestial movements. Five thousand years ago Chaldaean star-gazers believed they had learned the secrets of the heavens. Indeed, from their observatories in the Land of Two Rivers they had fixed the length of the year at 365 days, 6 hours, 15 minutes and 41 seconds—only 26 minutes and 26 seconds too long. And they knew that at intervals of eighteen years and eleven and a third days the earth, the moon, and the sun would be aligned, and thus they were able to predict solar eclipses.

The stars became one with the transcendental: the gazers became priests. Their alliance with the heavenly torches gave them power, and as the findings of the first eager searches were frozen into dogma intransigence fought hard against new sightings and facts. The central position of man in the cosmos was not questioned and was not allowed to be questioned. The stars existed for the sake of man, and at the same time they guided his fate. This egocentric viewpoint reached its culmination in the mystic faith of astrology, according to which each individual had his own star, to which he maintained a personal relationship. Out of this grew the beautiful but absurd idea that a star fell whenever a human being died.

In Pegasus, now grazing on the blue meadows over my head, there are a few double stars, just as there are in Aquarius and Capricorn. The Arabs gave them lucky names: the Luck of Rain, the Luck of Tents, the Luck of the Swallower, the Luck of the Camel Longing for Pastures, the Luck of Her Who Sows, the Luck of Lucks. Each name is a poem and reveals something about the content of luck. But such names also illustrate how the heavenly bodies existed for the sake of man. For him who swallows and for her who sows—even for a man's trusted camel longing for pastures.

Only after the light of pure thought had been lit in Hellas did the heavenly bodies come to be regarded as physical objects, susceptible of measurement and calculation. But here, too, daring had its limits, and the flame soon subsided. Even Apollo's priests had their dogmas. It is true that Anaximander seems to have been allowed to proclaim with impunity that the earth was a globe moving freely without support—earlier it had been visualized as a flat disc swimming in the ocean. But when Anaxagoras described the sun as "a glowing stone larger than the Peloponnesus" he was exiled from Athens for his heresy, just as Socrates would be forced to drain a cup of hemlock because he questioned certain ideas inherited from the bronze age.

And in the third century B. C., when that most magnificent of heretics Aristarchos of Samos hit on the idea that the earth moved around the sun, the idea was too dizzying and failed to win him many followers. Soon it was forgotten or smothered, and throughout the Middle Ages it was Aristotle who dictated the official cosmography: Tellus was the center of the universe, surrounded by globe-shaped shells to which the planets and the fixed stars were attached—and beyond them, empty space. Thus, egocentric cosmography was succeeded by a geocentric view, but even so the difference was infinitesimal. The crown of creation, man, remained secure in the center of creation.

When Canon Nicolaus Copernicus in Frauenburg, two thousand years after Aristarchos, snatched earth from the center of the universe and hurled it into its path around the sun, the thinking of man was ripe for one of its great revolutions. For Copernicus was not alone in returning to the thoughts from Samos, not alone in his revolt against the tyranny of Aristotle's opinions. Before the flames rose from the heretic's stake at Campo dei Fiori, Giordano Bruno had looked into "the multitude of worlds" with visionary clarity, and without the aid of instruments, without having discovered any new law of astronomy, had found that the earth, a planet among others, circled the sun. Galileo Galilei had been overwhelmed by what he saw in the first telescope (which his colleagues at the university of Padua regarded as an instrument of the devil), but before the curia he preferred to disavow his conviction—while murmuring something inaudible between his teeth. "The sun does not move," Leonardo da Vinci noted stealthily in one of his well-filled notebooks.

But Copernicus was the first to rearrange our part of the universe in an orderly way. He proceeded cannily, preventing even the omnipresent Inquisition from discovering what was going on until it was too late. It was not until seventy years after Copernicus on his death-bed had opened the first copy of his revolutionary work with quavering fingers, that the Church placed the volume on its "Index of Forbidden Books"—where it remained until as late as 1835. "That fool has turned the entire art of astronomy upside down," thundered Luther, himself a heretic, though on a smaller scale.

Yes, the quiet canon had crushed a cosmology and relegated the earth to a subordinate place in the solar system. That was bad enough, and yet it was only the first step along the path of revolution. The geocentric system had been replaced by a heliocentric one, but there remained the consolation that if our globe was not at the center of the universe, at least our sun was. Where we whirled on our double merry-go-round, first around the axis of Tellus, then around the sun, we forced the entire retinue of stars to keep us company.

Only our own age has completed the revolution and liberated the stars from the futile task of being our retinue. It has happened so fast and so recently that we are still a bit dizzy, incapable of accepting with our entire being what our intellect has been forced to concede.

With the aid of the Cyclops' eyes man has built to improve his own poor eyesight, with the giant telescopes on Mount Wilson and Mount Palomar, the star-gazers of today have untangled the shining veils of the Milky Way. Where the human eye can take in two thousand stars at most, the telescopes have found a hundred billion of them in our own galaxy alone. Our sun has been reduced to a rather ordinary star among billions of others, a star situated, moreover, in a rather uninteresting place far out on one of the spiral arms of the Milky Way, somewhere on one of the spokes of the big wheel of stars.

The center itself, the hub of the star wheel, is twenty-five thousand light years farther into the Milky Way. We cannot see it, even with our largest Cyclops' eyes. It is hidden behind shining curtains of the dust clouds that absorb most of the light of the stars. Our seat in the cosmic theater is a poor one, behind a curtain in the gallery. But radio telescopes, man's giant artificial ears, bear witness of violent activity behind the veils.

Near the southern horizon, just above the Urdadal peak, I have a feeling of glimpsing the constellation of Sagittarius. One of the weakly flickering lights that I perceive as a single star must be the star cloud, comprising billions of stars, in which the axis and the nucleus of the galaxy are lodged. It has taken twenty-five thousand years for light from the cloud to reach me this night. When it started from its source, Cro Magnon man was leaving his ice-age cave on the hunt for bison.

Our solar system is whirling around this distant center at a speed of about one hundred and forty miles a second. It takes two hundred million years to complete its tour around the center of the Milky Way—the cosmic year. When Tellus was last at the same point in the system, the first dinosaurs had begun lugging their armorplated bodies over the surface of the earth. Since the apelike man of Makapan arose, antelope club in hand, to scan the savanna, the sun with its nine planets and thirty satellites has completed only one two-hundredth part of its orbit around the center of the galaxy. During the span of a human life it has had time for only a minuscule step, three one-millionth parts of its orbit.

Man, as one latter-day star-gazer has put it, has become a frontiersman in his own galaxy and, beyond this galaxy, an overwhelming multitude of further Milky Ways, and others beyond them, strewn over the cosmic expanse. Some are loners, like our own Milky Way. Others are gathered in enormous clouds of stars—over Berenice's Hair there is a veil of eight hundred galaxies.

A strange spectacle, where nothing we see is simultaneous, where what we perceive as simultaneity comprises a span from relative proximity to the most distant past.

Our closest galactic neighbor in space, the only Milky Way outside our own that is visible with the naked eye, the Andromeda galaxy—named after the beautiful daughter of the Ethiopian king Cepheus, whom Pallas Athena gave a place among the stars—is two million light years from our own point of vantage. We see her as a diffuse spot of light in a place where she was before the first ice age started covering Tellus. With the telescope of today we can count thousands more galaxies than Galileo counted stars; with their aid we can photograph stellar systems so remote that their light has been on its way for three billion years. There the range of our lenses comes to an end, but from beyond the limits of what we can see, from beyond the cosmic horizon, modern radio telescopes capture the hum of worlds that are thought to be from six to eight billion light years away. What we hear may be the cosmic crash of galaxies colliding before our own planetary system emerged from a whirling mass of gases.

Within the dimension of depth in space and time that we can reach with our instruments, today's astronomers feel they can assume the existence of a hundred billion billion suns. These are figures beyond the limits of comprehension, and they become no more comprehensible if one tries to imagine counting them at a speed of one star a second, day and night. That would require three thousand six-hundred billion years, a span of time seven hundred times longer than our solar system has existed. Moreover, our instruments can never hope to capture more than a fraction of the total universe.

Somewhere among these myriads of glowing balls, formed on the cosmic potter's wheel, we are sitting in a highly accidental dark little spot, making history, sitting there with our temples and our towers of Babel, our dreams and our hunger for prestige, our super-bombs and our cold wars.

The celestial fireworks are still sparkling over the Urdadal peak. There is Sirius, there Orion. Sirius, the dog star, shining brightest of them all. Orion with the strange Betelgeuse, with a density only one thousandth of the earth's atmosphere and with Rigel shining with the force of eighteen thousands suns. The red eye of Taurus meets mine from a distance of fifty light years. Beyond it—billions of suns I cannot see.

To think that in this immensity, where everything is seething life and explosive force, man occupies any special position is a notion akin to the *hubris* against which the ancient Greeks warned. Nothing is unique at our frontier location in one galaxy among billions of them. Spectral analysis has demonstrated that even the remotest stars contain the same elements as earth. Hydrogen and oxygen, nitrogen, carbon and calcium—the building blocks of plants and animals on earth—exist everywhere in the universe. Life cannot be so strangely limited as to have gained its only foothold on our little shred of space in the vicinity of one of the hundred billion billion suns within our range of observation. In the great play of time and forces in the universe, inorganic substances must be transformed into life wherever chemical and physical conditions permit. All around the universe, in dark spots like our own, life must be seething—in different forms and stages of development.

Proof of life outside our own ball should soon be within

reach. Fallen meteorites, which we can interpret as splinters from exploded worlds, have been found to contain organized elements of a structure partly known on earth, partly arranged in other patterns—perhaps remnants of organisms in some antichamber of life.

We are likely to gain more reliable knowledge the day man sets foot on the bodies of our closest neighbors in the planetary system, whether they harbor dawning or ebbing life. The only risk is that officious rivalry to be first will lead to such poor preparation as to bring along micro-organisms from earth that may affect the processes in another world, depriving us of a cosmic opportunity to get acquainted with life in another phase of development, and perhaps nipping an evolution in the bud. Or that elements foreign to our earth are brought back from another planet, disrupting our own biological balance, perhaps giving rise to unknown epidemics.

We cannot expect to meet any rational beings or other organisms at a higher stage of development than our own when we visit our closest neighbors in space. Not on the rusty planet of the god of war, with its dry and dehumidified atmosphere from which the last showers must have fallen eons ago. Nor on that of the goddess of love, hiding coyly behind thick veils of carbon dioxide. And outside our own solar system we are not likely ever to go. From our own sun to the nearest star the distance is four light years—four light years separating us from the enigma of Alpha Centauri. If a man-made Aniara, the fictional space ship created by the Swedish writer Harry Martinson, were sent there at a speed of about seven miles a second (the velocity of today's rockets) it would require a hundred and twenty thousand years to reach its goal.

We will have to content ourselves with sending signals into space and hoping that somebody will intercept them and reply. The wavelength is obvious: the 21.1 centimeter band, the wavelength of hydrogen and thus of the universe.

Here and there in the world, astronomers are already sending regular signals toward distant stars. The odds on getting a reply are probably less than one in a billion. It would be a miracle if rational beings at our stage of development were to exist in the directions where we are searching and just happened to be listening at this very moment. Life there may be at an initial stage, or it may have destroyed itself, so that our signals bounce unheard off the burnt-out remnants of a radioactive world. Perhaps some other planet sent signals our way some million years ago—the man from Makapan did not catch them and the sender concluded that there was nobody home in these parts. If, that is, anyone were at all interested in our rather uninteresting spot in space.

Fantasies playing around for a moment, while the roof of heaven rises high over Visdal valley, and its arch rests on the mighty buttresses of the mountain.

We may never obtain proof that intelligent beings exist elsewhere in the universe—proof we can feel and touch. But the probability is overwhelming. Enormous odds can be posted. Thus, it would be an extremely cautious assumption that only one sun in a million has a planetary system, and that only one of these systems in a million houses a planet with conditions for life. Even so, this would mean a hundred million bearers of life within the portion of space we can reach with our instruments. In some of them—say only one in a thousand, which would mean in a hundred thousand worlds—evolution may have forged intelligent creatures on its anvil.

No matter how much of an accident man may be on his planet, the fact remains that he has emerged from the salts and juices of the earth in the same way as the fly's bane and the earthworm. On other life-bearing planets, too, evolution must have led to beings capable of forging the metals of their planet into tools, of thinking, and of having cosmic concepts.

That they would be like us, even though formed out of the same elements, hardly seems probable. We, the frontiersmen of the Milky Way, cannot be the prototype for other rational beings in the universe. We must consider it probable, then, that beings with sensory organs unknown to us, perhaps inconceivable to us, exist elsewhere in the universe. Our eyes, those fine instruments that enable us to look out toward the mass of stars, can only perceive an infinitesimal portion of the large spectrum of rays—what appears to us as "visible light." But even the faceted eye of the common housefly probably perceives another portion. Perhaps there are—beyond Mira Ceti, "the wondrous one," or in the region of the Luck of Her Who Sows—creatures with organs capable of registering phenomena totally unknown to us and of providing an explanation of the world that is entirely different from our own. But in such matters we shall probably never advance beyond assumptions and premonitions, bound as we are to the planet that created us, and separated as we are by such huge distances from other possibly inhabited worlds.

The origin of it all hides behind even more impenetrable nebulosae from past eons. Perhaps one day we shall be able to form a clearer picture of the process of cosmic creation. Perhaps, however, we will find that for every new clarity we gain new enigmas and difficulties.

The further our telescopes reach, the more we recede backwards in time. We see stars as they appeared billions of years ago. We see spots where they shone then, while in reality they have whirled on in the enormous pattern of movement of the universe.

The astronomers of today are struck by observations pointing to an expanding universe. The farther out you get, it seems, the more isolated the beacons of space seem to glow, and the more rapidly individual stars and galaxies appear to recede—finally at the fantastic speed of more than sixty thousand miles per second, or one third the speed of light. Radio telescopes are supplying us with the evidence for this: the more distant the sources from which we receive signals, the more the rays move into the red band of the spectrum. And a movement away from us—according to the laws of physics —would yield such red signals.

From these observations some astronomers have postulated an epoch billions of years ago when the entire mass of the universe would have been compressed into a primordial atom of unfathomable weight and density—at least one hundred million tons per cubic centimeter. Then in a big bang—the only one that could really merit being called *the* bang of all time—the potential universe enclosed in the primordial atom would have been exploded and its ingredients hurled out in a cosmic square dance that is still continuing. According to this theory, the stars are merely smoldering embers from that great explosion and are, if we project this theory into the future, all destined for eventual extinction. All energy evaporated, the universe emptied, time itself would come to a halt.

To a layman, this theory seems very unsatisfactory. It begs the very questions that a primitive cosmography tried to resolve by imagining a *demiurgos,* with his *"fiat,"* prior to the beginning of everything. Of course, we cannot properly seek a meaning in the universe according to our personal lights. But if everything were moving from a definite beginning to a definite moment of annihilation, then the whole adventure would still be one of cosmic meaninglessness. As interpreters of the cosmos we are still first-graders; we have spelled our way through the first pages of the giant book, but if we try to peek further ahead in its pages we may easily misunderstand the difficult script. Perhaps the red shift in the spectrum, which has been taken as evidence for the theory of creation all at once in a big bang, has some quite different explanation. Someone has suggested the possibility, for example, that light on its way through the billions of years has lost some of its energy, gotten a bit tired, and therefore shifted towards the longer and less energy-laden wavelengths that the spectrograph paints red.

How infinitely more fascinating and meaningful is another vision that has been opened to us by the new astronomy: the vision of a continuing process of creation, without limits in time and space.

Space between the stars is not, after all, quite so empty as was believed even so recently as a couple of decades ago. The discovery of great quantities of dust and matter moving in interstellar space opens perspectives as dizzying as the discovery of new galaxies. Even if the density is inconceivably low—lower than the thinnest vacuum we are able to create on earth—the aggregate amount of dust is still inconceivably large. Within our own Milky Way alone it would correspond to three hundred trillion earths, and within all of visible space it would amount to as much as all the matter in all the stars.

This dust, thinner than a whisper, contains the same elements we know from earth, from the sun, and from the stars. Hydrogen, the primary building element of the universe, is the predominant ingredient. In some parts of space the dust has collected into giant clouds that we can photograph. Even if a single human life is much too brief to follow the processes, we can sense that we may be glimpsing the cradles of new worlds in which the baking of future stars has begun.

There is flaming Orion, with its gaseous nebula lit by the brilliance of Rigel. Out of its whirls, in coming ages, new stars will perhaps take shape, shining as brightly as our own sun. Some astronomers think that during the last billion years several hundred stars have already been born out of this gaseous cloud. In the Magellanic cloud, an appendix to our own Milky Way, which the first circumnavigator of the earth sighted under the Southern Cross, the creation of stars appears to be proceeding a great speed. And the same spectacle is being repeated wherever we turn the lenses of our telescopes.

The death of stars, easier to observe than their birth, has always captured the imagination of man. He has gazed in wonder at the novas as they light up, shining for a few weeks only to pale again—cosmic bombs blowing up a solar system and hurling its contents into space. Or the supernovas, those extensive giants among stars that live a brief life and die a splendid death in a sea of flames hundreds of millions times more brilliant than the sun.

When I was my companion's age, I was fascinated by stories of how Chinese chroniclers and rock-carving Indians in Arizona had conveyed to posterity a message about a supernova bursting on the firmament. Today we know that the explosion took place five thousand years before the Chinese scholars and the simple Indians of the prairies, living close to the stars, captured a glimpse of its light. In the meantime, two hundred generations had lived and died, cultures had emerged and disappeared. To this day we can see the dust cloud from the explosion in the nebula of Cancer. It spreads not unlike the blue smoke rising from my pipe.

The death of stars is going on everywhere. A score of explosions are registered every year in our own Milky Way alone. In the nebulosae we can read the obituaries of stars that have shone and expired.

But the matter of which those exploding stars had been built—stars that may have given light and heat to living creatures on faraway planets—that matter is not consumed. How fascinating it is to remind oneself that nothing in nature can be destroyed. A star may be blown into atoms, the atoms may be dissolved into protons and electrons, matter may be turned into radiation, but the elemental building-blocks remain, and radiation can again be condensed into matter. The dust thrown off by dying stars may join other masses of dust in space and may someday be part of new stars and planetary systems.

Thus, on a cosmic scale, the same cycle develops that we know on our own insignificant planet: the cycle of birth, youth, aging, and death—and death itself the prerequisite of new life.

The perspectives opened by the new cosmology make the head swim. It reduces the "crown of the universe" to complete cosmic insignificance—a creature bound to a dark little spot that is smaller than one three-hundred-thousandth part of the star around which it rotates. He is only a frontiersman in a galaxy sending a hundred billion other stars spinning in space, a galaxy lost among billions of others within his range of observation. He has been assigned a walk-on part in a cosmic drama which allows his species to perform for no more than a fraction of a second of eternity. In the same perspective as the stars, the dogma of the presumed preeminence of man surely evaporates.

And yet, the more we shrink, the wider our horizons become. No matter how insignificant our role, the cosmic drama in which we are allowed to perform for a moment is magnificent. Our mind, once it is awakened inside a cranium that used to be a cavity for wordless perception, enables us to follow a part of the drama, thus allowing us to see ourselves as portions of totality.

Since the entire universe is built from the same basic elements, since hydrogen and oxygen, carbon, and calcium are building-blocks of the galaxies and the interstellar dust clouds as well as of the thin film of life on our own globe, man himself is made of the raw material of the stars. Nature produces its enormous variety by combining just a few elementary particles in many different ways. They take shape in mountains and waters, in creeping heather and birds of paradise, in suns and men. My brain, which on this star-lit mountain night tries to capture some of the drama, albeit imperfectly and piecemeal, was formed out of the same elementary particles as the brilliant dust cloud in Orion. My eyes, registering the celestial spectacle, was formed out of the same elements as the red eye of Taurus, the enormous Aldebaran. We are made of such stuff as stars are made of.

Our planetary system was formed out of a whirling cloud of dust and gases. In this cloud there must have been particles hurled into space by some star explosion. Consequently, the earth and everything on it must contain elements that were once part of other stars and planets. Thus the individual human being carries within him the very elements that once helped build a star in some other sky than ours. At a distant time in the future, a few billion years from now, the sun will swell until it takes in all the inner planets, roasting the earth and turning its oceans into steam. Then, in the shape of a panting nova, it will burst and dissolve into an interstellar dust cloud. Particles that once were a human being will whirl around within the cloud, only to take part eons ahead, perhaps, in the building of new worlds, with their mountains, their water, and perhaps even their living creatures.

Somewhere from the cosmic expanse came the elements out of which my temporary personality was formed. Somewhere they will one day whirl on. Never before have they been combined in the way that gave rise to this particular "me," and never again will they return in the same combination. My fleeting self has never existed before and will never exist again, but if the smallest component parts of matter cannot be annihilated, protons and electrons from my material person will still be taking part in building new matter, organic or inorganic, long after the earth I am treading has ceased to exist.

Nothing could inspire more solemnity than the picture evoked by the new cosmology. Instead of occupying the special position we used to assign to ourselves, we form part of the dizzying totality of space and time. We are in the universe and the universe is in us. Compared to this picture of the cosmos, the old explanations of creation and reincarnation, however beautiful in their symbolism, appear crude and awkward.

Surmounting the delusion of Tellus as the center of the universe, with a retinue of stars created just for the sake of man, has been slow work. Even today dogmas that are not many cuts above the most primitive of cosmic explanations are accorded the deepest bows in many quarters. Space probes and atom splitters notwithstanding, venerable superstitions have adherents comparable, in some ways, to the present-day cave dwellers in New Guinea, who believe that airplanes are works of the gods and faithfully light fires in their mountains at night to guide the gods as they travel about in their humming celestial vehicles. We are able to accept new facts in the abstract, it seems, but the cosmic expanse has been opened to our gaze too fast for us to adapt our minds to the new picture.

The revolt against the tyranny of Aristotle's thought refused to subside. In the same way, a new view of the world, based on the new cosmology, will have to force itself on us. Is anything else possible but that we shall again come closer to the stars—in a great new realization of "belonging," of our being, despite our infinite smallness, components in a universal context?

As the stars fade over the Urdadal peak and night wind rustles through willow brushes and creeping heather, the mind catches a glimpse of some of the questions about what all this may mean. Will it necessarily give rise to a revolution in man's thinking, one that may have consequences more earth shaking than those of any previous revolution in the history of human thought? Is it possible that all this can have no effect on the ways in which man organizes his own community—in his marginal home on the outskirts of a galaxy?

4

". . . and the solar wind plays . . ."

MORNING IN THE MOUNTAINS—FRESHLY WASHED,
bathed in sunlight. We are resting on rocks gray with lichen,
alongside waters that make it easy for us to rest.

There seems to be water everywhere around us—between the rocks, running over shiny ledges, underneath tufts
and wads of moss. It slurps and gurgles, rustles and ripples.
It comes out of the ground, from yesterday's rain, and from
Visbre glacier. It plays in a thousand and one rills and eddies
converging on the brook farther down the valley, eventually
to find its way to the Skagerrak.

Not all of the glittering molecules will get that far. Some
are soon to be lifted again by the sun, destined to return
later in fresh drizzles and downpours. Some will serve in the
metabolism of a salmon trout or an aspen tree. Some may
disappear through a powerhouse tunnel and lend man a part
of their energy.

We started early. The mountain morning goes fast, and
you have to get up betimes if you hope to know it. At dawn

an ochre-toned hue spreads over the slopes to the west, flowing downward at a visible pace. It shoves the shadows before it and then, suddenly, the mountain is there—a cool grayish brown, silver-striped with hanging brooks. Up around the crests where sky begins, the air seems fluorescent; down in the valley where we are walking a myriad of drops glisten on leaves and straws.

The hillside to the east is still dark, waiting for Earth to turn another few degrees to admit the sun. There, over a black cauldron, is the Spitra fall, hanging freely over a hole it has been digging for itself. Now and then it is caught by a gust of wind and tossed across the cauldron, making the water rise again as a cloud over the mountain ridge. Even so, the Spitra receives quite a few dippers of water to send down to the sea.

And here we are now, lying down for a morning rest among a few boulders in one of those spots where rivers are born. My companion takes in his fill of mountain. But he is also practical and he knows the uses of the rippling mountain water—fresh coffee and a brisk rub-down.

Over our heads—the sun! You can almost feel its interplay with the mountain, the glacier, the ubiquitous water.

After all, that is how it really is, though to an extent and in a complexity that our senses cannot fully grasp. Yet I do know that the sun is much more than the isolated glowing ball that my eye perceives. Its gaseous cover reaches far outside the visible circle, gradually thinning out until it merges imperceptibly with space. And from the titanic eruptions and the wild magnetic storms in the sun, fast-moving particles are constantly being hurled out into the sea of space.

Only the smallest fraction of them are able to reach the tiny vestige of the original gas cloud that we call Tellus. But even at that the solar wind brings us a ton and a half of solar matter, mostly hydrogen nuclei, every second. We capture five million tons of cosmic matter per year—all from the solar wind. It is true that this amount causes our earth to grow by no more than a thousandth of a gram per square centimeter in a thousand years, but in such matters of cosmic cooperation there is an abundance of time. Combined with oxygen, the amount of hydrogen that will have reached us from space in three billion years would be enough to fill all our oceans.

More immediately, there is some of this solar matter in the black coffee, made from fresh mountain water, that my companion is handing me just now.

Along with the solar wind the electrons also come like astronauts in a great hurry, capable of making the trip from pole to pole in less than a second. When they emerge in large armadas, we are captivated by the splendor of the aurora borealis. Sometimes we see entire meteors from space. Then we talk of shooting stars—of lyrids, perseids, leonids.

For Tellus is no isolated body in the universe. It is our celestial home, to be sure, but it has no given place and no firm frontiers; it is only a spot in the solar system, one whose rarefied gas is gradually absorbed in the cosmos. In the spring of creation, earth must have emitted large quantities of methane and gaseous ammonia into space. Even today it emits gases from the outer layers of its atmosphere, while at the same time absorbing other elements from outside.

In one of his conversations with Eckermann, Goethe spoke of visualizing earth and its atmosphere as a living being in the constant process of exhalation and inhalation. That vision has been confirmed by today's scientists. They can demonstrate that our globe is truly in constant exchange with the universe. Our earth (and we ourselves) was first built from the raw material of the stars; now, with the solar wind and with cosmic radiation, it receives new building materials from space every minute. Thus, our relationship with the universe is here and now. We are sharing in the enormous forces that work between the stars.

The sun pours forth heat and the solar wind plays.

Even at a very early stage of his being man must have seen the sun as the giver of life. At first, perhaps, it was a vague feeling somewhere below the conscious level—but later the name of the sun became one of the earliest of articulated words, along with *you* and *I, mother* and *father.*

It is easy to understand how, in the most diverse cultures and in religions at various stages of development, the sun could become an object of worship. How much more reasonable was a sun god than the gods man has created, in his vanity, after his own image—gods gorging themselves on roast pork in Valhalla, loving and quarreling on Mount Olympus, or sending flashes out of the clouds over the Sinai desert.

There we see the solar sign in gray rock carvings—an age-old magic symbol. There Pharaoh, himself a god, greeting his alter ego, the rising sun, after cleansing himself in the House of the Morning. There Aztecs, working for generations to construct temples that would lift their priests just a few dozen feet closer to the glowing celestial body. There Apollo driving his sun-chariot across the sky, while devotees below praise the sun ray as the *plektron* of his divine lyre. And there, in a battle on Roman soil between the sun god Mithras and Christ—suddenly ended by imperial decree in the christening of the empire, while the church was paganized—again we see the sign of the sun, now as a halo around the head of the Nazarene. And is there not something of the sun god also to be found in the flames of our Scandinavian Mayday and midsummer bonfires—an ancient Indo-European ritual of sun worship—and in the fire that is to burn perpetually in the temples of the Parsees as a symbol of Ahura Mazda?

As one walks in the flowing sun along a Norwegian mountain valley it is possible for the mind to turn suddenly to certain ancient temple paintings from the banks of the

Nile—paintings in which the rays of the sun end in a multitude of small hands strewing life over the earth. In their naive charm they seem to show just what latter-day scientists have found—that the flaming ball of gas with the atomic reactor in its interior is the omnipotent creator of all life on earth, the father of ours which art in heaven.

Now the sun is groping with warm hands in a valley of the home of the giants. It feels doubly good after yesterday's hours of freezing hail and snow. The creeping heather, refreshed by yesterday's precipitation and urged on by the sun, fills the air with volatile scents. Even the ice ranunculi take on a warm hue.

We have left the site of our early morning break and are working our way towards the forty-five hundred foot level along the slope of the Tverrbotthorn. We have left behind the pyramid of Semmelholstind, and ahead of us Kyrkja raises her spire. It is newly whitewashed against a bluish black background, and the point glistens. Give the sun a bit more time and it will scrape away the whitewash down toward the base.

As you walk here, sensing how some of the billion billion horsepower of the sun are working all around you, it may be tempting to try to capture some glimpses of the great panorama from the moment life made its first start in the primordial sea until the present day and age.

A naked planet, sterile and solemnly desolate, closer to the glowing central body than earth is now. It rotates rapidly; the day is only a third as long as it is now, and so is the year. The rapid rotation gives strength to the winds. Violent hurricanes sweep the surface of the earth, and chaotic thunderstorms rage day and night. There are dense vapors of ammonia, methane, and carbon dioxide over the globe, but as yet no blanket of oxygen, no layer of ozone to filter the ultraviolet rays from the sun. The rays bombard the globe and play in the oceans.

The sun empties its semen into the womb of the sea. Rays that may someday extinguish all life become the promoters of life. Slowly, in the course of perhaps a billion years or so, inorganic substances begin to dissolve and to form new chemical compounds. Their various possibilities of survival are tested unendingly. Many compounds are discarded; others stand the test. The cosmic laboratory begins to produce proteins and other organic substances, and they proliferate and fill the shallow ocean with nutrients. It is not quite life yet—but life at the threshold of life. The first step has been taken on a road that will lead to mice and men, poets and potentates.

We know today that this is probably about the way it happened. American scientists have recently tried to reconstruct a fragment of the workshop of creation as it has been visualized in theory. They have produced an artificial primordial sea with vapors of ammonia, methane, and water, and caused artificial lightning to flash and ultraviolet rays to work on inorganic matter in it. And lo, in the test tube there emerged precursors of the proteins that build life. Other experiments have yielded building blocks of the chlorophyll of plants and the haemoglobin of our own blood. Thus it has been found possible to perform at least the prelude to creation in an ordinary test tube.

In this way we have provided ourselves with one of the proofs we sought of life in other worlds. What must have happened on earth, what we ourselves have begun to be able to achieve in our test tubes, is a process that over billions of years must have occurred and is even now occurring all around the universe. If so, life is indeed the realization of a cosmic principle.

Once started, the process cannot be stopped. Atoms

have been joined into molecules, molecules into cells. What used to be chemistry becomes life. One day a cell splits. The old cell does not cease to exist—it leaves no corpse—but it becomes two. With fissiparous reproduction the order of the day, the evolutionary process has begun.

The two new cells, which are nothing but the old cell in duplicate, become four, the four become eight, the eight, sixteen. But at no point does the original cell cease to exist. There is no death, only constant rejuvenation—one of the heavenly dreams of latter-day man realized in the early amoeba. It is a world in which individual and collective are one, and a world in which the struggle for existence has not yet begun in earnest.

But then the reverse process starts to occur. Cells begin to join. Primitive organisms, for which we have no name, begin to take shape. One may surmise that the scene is one of shallow bays where solid, fluid, and gaseous substances —earth, water, and air—had a rendezvous, and where the sun's ultraviolet rays could play freely in the primordial broth—mixing, joining, mutating. It is certainly not a matter of an isolated event, but one of repeated biological experiments. But somewhere in these small lumps of protein are the seeds that will flower one day in the mighty initial chords of Beethoven's Symphony of Fate, in Plato's dialogues, in Raphael's madonnas.

Just as there has never been a clear borderline between dead and living matter, so there is no absolute line of demarcation between plant and animal life. Both streams of evolution have the same original source. However, the earliest organisms, of which it is impossible to say whether they are animals or plants, specialize into plants and start to fill the seas. Primitive blue algae, which tell of their existence in fossils almost two billion years old, help us with the dates.

The globe itself is still seeking its shape. The contours of sea and land are in constant flux. Breakers hurl themselves against naked rocks, saline swells roll towards a slimy no man's land. Maritime plants washed ashore on marshy beaches try to absorb the salts of the soil and the gases of the air. Some plants survive the change of environment and begin to wander into the interior. This opens up a new world. Hitherto naked, virgin continents are now to be draped in a green veil. This veil will create conditions suitable for animal life, for plants have a primary ability that animals will never acquire—the ability to bring about a kind of co-operation between the sun and the mineral masses of the earth. In their chlorophyll, plants store energy received from the violent atomic processes of the sun; they capture carbon and water and mineral salts, and out of it all they manufacture complicated nutrients—sugar, starches, cellulose. Animal life is to choose a less laborious way—that of using plants as a short-cut by which to utilize the salts of the sea and the soil.

Once plant life has established itself, the time is ripe for the other current of evolution. Certain primitive organisms begin to specialize in sponging off plants, consuming nutrients that the plants have collected and produced. Thus animal life begins to take shape. First in the sea—so salty and nutritious, the womb of all living things. But as lichen, mushrooms, and ferns wander inland, a paradise is being prepared for the animal when it is ready to follow.

Among the more complex organisms, plant or animal, reproduction by splitting in two becomes increasingly less satisfactory, and nature "experiments" and builds reproductive devices into them. Nature is profligate with opportunities—spores, sperm, eggs spew forth, whirling, steaming, passing on the original seeds of life.

And with these new ways of reproducing life, death enters on the scene. When two individuals of the same species join and produce a third, perpetual existence on the pattern of the amoeba ceases to be possible. But basically the difference is not great. Considering the existence of the individual in a larger framework, death means only that certain worn-out auxiliary organs are discarded, whereas the seed of life itself continues on in fresh individuals. Thus the individual becomes a temporary passinger between two stations in existence. He may leave his mark in fossils and clay tablets, in saber teeth and mammoth tusks, in sonatas or in ruins, but as an individual he will never return, once the auxiliary organs he has supplied with life have been used up. Nevertheless, the seed of life in the primordial cell lives on and on.

Death is the premise of the constant renewal of the forms of life. The amoeba remained essentially the same individual no matter how it proliferated, whereas death means continuous variations, continuous selection. It lets individuals and even species perish, while other and more advanced bearers of life replace them. Death makes evolution itself possible.

The world of the amoeba was a static one. The world in which death joins reproduction becomes a moving world, a world of struggle. With death comes the struggle for existence and the merciless selectivity of nature. In the battle for food, the better-equipped are the more likely to survive and reproduce.

The connection is so ironclad as to permit the assumption that the same drama must be repeated wherever life may have emerged. Nowhere in the universe can we expect the human dreams of a Shangri-la to be realized. Not beyond Mira Ceti or beyond the Luck of Her Who Sows. If the life we know is truly the realization of a cosmic principle, we must assume that the struggle for existence and the process of natural selection is a universal law.

Creation becomes testing and weeding. Individuals and species compete for the food resources. Some species acquire a suitable shape and equipment early and are able to live on through millions of years. Thus fish, which acquired their sleek shape before any mammals had yet been born, survive, while their pelagic relatives, the three-eyed trilobites, perish. Insects, which may again possess the world if man makes it unsuitable for higher forms of life—insects, which account for seven tenths of the million animal species now in existence and which, though diminutive individually, are believed to weigh collectively three times as much as all the mammals, fish, reptiles, and birds on earth—insects were also ready for the game very early, and they were the first animal forms to populate the continents, gathering their nourishment from the plants on the ground. But billions of other animal forms blunder into blind alleys and are mustered out as unfit.

In certain places truly fabulous evolutionary possibilities exist. From out of the Devonian sea, some three hundred million years ago, certain fish move on to marshy beaches and shallow puddles. When the puddles go dry, mass death takes most of the emigrants. But some of them have air-bladders, which begin to serve as lungs. They can utilize the oxygen of the air. They begin an amphibian existence, now in water, now on land.

A coelecanth with strong anterior fins crawls further and further up on land in search of food. He adapts himself slowly to this new and adventurous environment and even begins climbing trees. The age of reptiles has begun.

The family tree grows new branches.

A climbing lizard stretches its forelegs into flight, first from branch to branch, then farther, stretching its neck, until one day it streaks through the sky in the plow formation of the wild goose, croaks hoarsely in a raven, sails in a sea tern, excels in splendor in a bird of paradise—but deep in the vigilant black eye of the bird there lurks the cold gleam of the reptile.

Another branch leads to the mammals, latecomers but having a wide-ranging potential for variety. Some begin to swell with weight, but this does not guarantee survival in the struggle for existence, for just as the largest stars soon consume their reserves of energy and rush headlong into stellar death, so many wandering mountains of flesh and armor blunder into the difficulties that accompany all greatness.

Indeed, the smaller and more agile mammals seem to have a better chance of development. Out of a forerunner the size of a pig the elephant grows. A fleet-footed runner no bigger than a hare becomes a thoroughbred in the stable of the Aga Khan or a broad-beamed mare hauling a brewer's wagon. From a creature the size of a squirrel a jungle ape evolves, now devoting himself to his venereal pastimes, now aggressively guarding his territory. And then one day an ape-man steps out of the jungle, stretching high to scan the savanna.

Thus man enters the teeming panorama of species. His erect posture, which frees the anterior extremities for the manufacture of tools and weapons, is an evolutionary novelty as decisive as the transformation of the lizard's foot into the wing of a bird. His other revolutionary innovation is the new brain. Biologically, it is nothing but an enlarged version of the brain of the primate—the biological difference is so small, indeed, as to make a comparison between the existence of man and the naked and threatened survival of the jungle ape seem rather ominous. Yet it is by use of his larger brain that man has been able to split atoms and peer through the myriad of light years toward distant worlds.

Man is a newcomer—one so newly arrived on the scene that he ought by rights to be at the very beginning of his evolutionary career. If we imagine the history of the earth compressed within the span of an earth year, from the moment the gaseous cloud began to congeal until this day, the first forms of life would appear in midsummer. The first manlike forms would enter the scene shortly before midnight on December 30. And the entrance cue for Homo sapiens would be just ten minutes before New Year's Eve.

The coelecanth, the broom-finned fish, made the adventure possible. We are still carrying his mark, as are our relatives among land animals—including the ones that have returned to the sea. Those strong frontal fins, which enabled him to crawl out of the puddle on the beach, were supported by five strong fin bones—a legacy to his descendants, for whom they had many uses: climbing and flying, swimming and walking, tearing up food. They are found in the toes of the frog and the mouse and the elephant, in the paw of the lion, in the frontal fin of the whale and the hand of the monkey. They were in Paganini's hand as he moved the bow over his Stradivarius, and in Einstein's hand as he wrote down the formula that bared the slumbering energy of the atoms.

That same fin is in my hand as I light my pipe to indicate to my companion that here at a small tarn in Semmedalsmunnen, from where we have a view toward Langvatnet and up to the Högvagl peak, it is time for another rest. We have been trudging along briskly ever since rounding Kyrkja, and this small body of water, icy blue where the mountain shadows it but a heavenly pale elsewhere, seems to have been waiting just for us.

My companion has put down his rucksack and continued up the slope a bit. Now he points eagerly upward. A buzzard appears, with wings spread black against the cloud banks about to rise over the rim of the nearest mountain. He flows in even flight, with a profile that is puzzling in its similarity to that of the royal eagle. His call is a rough craw-craw, sounding as if it came to us straight out of the rock.

Now some higher-pitched craw-craws are heard—his nest must be nearby. And there, suddenly, a small dark bundle flaps against the side of the mountain, rises, falls, dives in the wind and is lifted by it. A feathered reptile in its first attempt at flight.

The old buzzard continues his circling flight and his coarse cry—perhaps he has caught sight of a couple of intruders in his territory. Then again, he may be on quite different business, leaving him no time for two small figures by a mountain pool. You can never be certain just how a buzzard looks at human beings.

Man can just barely comprehend what is closest to him in space, in time, in the evolutionary span. Evolution has placed him somewhere between the infinitely large and the infinitely small. He happens to be as much larger than a hydrogen atom as the sun, with its nine hundred and ninety-nine thousandths of the mass of our planetary system, is larger than man.

He lives wedged-in between two of the Chinese boxes of existence. The boxes are vaguely transparent. He can discern a little of what is in the ones closest in size outside and inside, but the farther he peers in both directions, the more blurred is the view, the less sure he can be of what he sees. He can augment his poor eyesight somewhat by the use of telescopes and microscopes, but he is still unable to reach either the outermost box of the infinitely large or the innermost of the infinitely small.

Man knows a little bit about the universe of the galaxies, and a little bit about the universe of the atoms, in which electrons chase around their nucleus at the same relative distance as a planet around its mother star. And in theories, symbols, and the arcane language of formulas he can capture some of what his senses fail to perceive directly. He even feels that he can sense something of the law-governed interplay between the largest and the smallest, but he can no more understand it fully than can the ant crawling over Einstein's book interpret his formulas. The dimensions are either too immense or too small. Every new look into the macrocosm discloses new riddles and amorphities, and at the other extreme, man's senses cannot detect the smallest components of matter and life. Receding beyond the governing "laws" he thinks he has discovered there are always new obscurities and contradictions.

What hamstrings him ultimately is the fact that he is himself part of the totality he is trying to explore. The visible world, as Plato knew, is a prison. But man, at his frontier post, is not only a product of, but also an actor in, a stupendous play of balances.

Stand on a mountain slope, warming yourself in the sun before it is devoured by the rising cloud banks. Wash your lungs with pure mountain air. You are taking part, no matter how hidden your role, in the immense barter of nature. Everywhere plants are inhaling carbon dioxide and breaking it down into nutrients (with the aid of solar energy). At the same time they are exhaling oxygen that they freed from the water. You inhale that same oxygen and exhale carbon dioxide—freeing it to be absorbed again by the plants. The circulation is absolute. Plants not only provide nourishment for your digestion but also the very air you breathe. All oxygen in the atmosphere has come from those plants, and without them no animal life of the kind we know could ever exist. You give them, in turn, not only fertilizer for their roots but also part of the air required by their respiratory apparatus. What one line of evolution emits as consumed is picked up by the other as nourishment—"the breath of life."

Stand and fill your lungs with air. With every breath you inhale a thousand billion billion atoms. A few million billion of them are long-living argon atoms that are exhaled within the second and dispersed with the winds. Time mixes them and has been mixing them for a long time. Some of them may have visited Buddha or Caesar, or even earlier paid a call on the man from Makapan.

Not your lungs alone but the whole of your body takes part in the symbiosis. Your body is no more an isolated whole than the sun or the earth are. It merges with its environment, constantly giving off atoms and taking up fresh ones. In the course of a year it consumes many more atoms than there are drops of water in this mountain 'tarn. Some of the fresh atoms that you absorb may once have helped build up Socrates or his judges, the cave artist of Lascaux, a saber-toothed tiger, or perhaps a buzzard like the one still circling over our head. The individual, after all, is only a temporary arrangement of ingredients that existed before him and will continue to exist forever, in one guise or another. And many ingredients make only fleeting guest appearances.

August Strindberg saw the lines of fish, the orbits of stars, and sea-shells and plants in the contours of a woman's body. Perhaps there is a form per se as a universal theme based on the variation and repetition of what serves the purpose—a fascinating subject for esthetic speculation. But what we know today scientifically is that the building blocks of stars, fish, shells, and plants are all in our own bodies. If the politicians have yet to learn that the world is truly one and indivisible, at least the biologists have learned it.

The pilgrimage of species—the metamorphosis from the protein molecule and the solitary cell (via algae and fish), amphibians, reptiles, and modest little mammals) to our own species, Homo sapiens. The seed of life in the priordial cell, awakened by the sun in the slime of the primordial sea, living on and on in the temporary shell you call "self" and in all the beings around you. Is it possible to watch this panorama, testifying to the unity of life, without becoming emotionally aware of your own intimate relation with all else that lives and breathes?

For in all our rationality—which so often leads us to such irrational deeds—we also hoard, deep within the innermost cells of our primordial brain, a legacy of emotional experiences and behavioral lines inherited from earlier forms of existence—a legacy reaching further back in time than Makapan, back to the immense tidal wave of life that so recently swept man on to the beach of consciousness. Just as our hand still bears the mark of the coelecanth, so on a deeper level this legacy ties us to the other forms of life, past and present. And each form of existence, whether that of an individual or that of a species, is something fleeting, existing in its peculiar form for only a moment. The present is not a state of being but a slide, a transition between past and future. Creation is an unfinished symphony, a drama on which no curtain falls. All is change and re-creation, and everything is new under the sun.

There are clouds across the sun now, but the solar wind is at play nevertheless, making its vital contribution to the continuous process of re-creation. Through the fine dust, invisible to our eyes but with us nevertheless, continually falling from space and entering all living beings, we take part in an unceasing cosmic re-creation. We are participants not merely in the big barter of our own globe but also in a cosmic symbiosis.

All this we can know, or at least sense—and that will have to suffice. We can proceed no further. The basic properties of atoms seem to be the same, no matter what part they take in building nature, and the same basic events must be taking place inside our brain as we think and feel, yearn and desire, as are taking place in the cosmos as a whole. But as soon as we ask what all this *means*, we are confounded by seemingly insurmountable barriers.

Far out on a spiral arm of a galaxy, man emerged as a species through which evolution tested the possibilities of the big brain and allowed the cosmos to see itself. What the test is going to reveal we cannot know—it started so recently.

But since the test began—in the course of a time interval that is infinitesimal compared to the eons it took to bring us here—this brain has completed a cycle that now gives rise to disturbing questions. Somewhere in the warm primordial sea the power of the sun brought forth what would one day result in man. But now man himself has released cosmic forces, man himself has begun to copy the processes of the sun and to create his own suns. What destiny do they carry inside themselves? A being formed out of the raw materials of the stars has himself placed stars in the sky—over the Kalahari desert and the canyons of the metropolis. What is their message?

The other wild beasts, which once sharpened the vigilance of man's eye, are no longer of any real danger to him. We are beginning to be able to control the pestilence of epidemic diseases. The stars of space do not seem to threaten us—our sun, which in billions of years of transforming hydrogen into helium has used up only a tiny fraction of its reserves, will presumably shine on for billions of years in future, thus allowing the solar wind to continue to play over our globe.

And yet mankind finds itself confronted by a threat worse than any to which Homo sapiens has ever been exposed in the past.

The threat to man comes from man himself.

Or?

Towards evening the sun-raised water molecules return. The clouds are dissolved in a quiet drizzle. It does not fall— it is simply there. At times the clouds drag so low that you are inside them, pressed by millions of little drops that you can hardly see but certainly feel. We decide to spend the night at Olavsbu, a self-service hut under the Rauddal ridge.

There are some young people already in the hut when we arrive—a few from Eidsbugaren, some from Gjendebu, others from Skogadalsböen. They have never met before but all are immediately on a friendly basis as members of a community of the mountain. They help each other to get firewood, build a fire, and prepare food; they hang their wet clothes around the stove to dry without getting in each other's way; they decide who will sleep where, whether on cots or on the floor. It is all accomplished naturally, without ceremony, in a simple joy of life far from noise and affectation.

Suddently I find that I have to smile at my ruminations just now. Man a threat to man himself? No, it is all too absurd.

5

". . . the world conquered by the hunter on his naked feet . . ."

TUFTS OF CLOUD ARE CROWDING EACH OTHER around the Rauddal ridge, like a wreath at its crest. Each tuft seems reluctant to tear itself away.

The morning feels bleak after a night lashed by rain, but the sun is attempting to pierce the cracks between the lively clouds, and for long periods it is successful.

We follow the brook through Rauddal valley—as lively and unpredictable as the clouds. Time and again the stream widens into wrinkled tarns of shimmering green.

We are in no hurry and stop whenever we wish. We follow a whirl of water at its work, noting how it has dug cavities in the rock and polished them. We peer at a mountain skua skating through the air with the elegant refinement of a sea tern. We listen to a sound reminiscent of that of a partridge until it is drowned out by a bluethroat starting a new composition. We bend over a gentian or a diapensia or perhaps only a bunchberry, pathetically black inside its white involucre. In this vicinity the rock is full of limestone and these plants can thrive all the way up to the snow line.

Somewhere Linnaeus speaks of the observation of nature as "the highest peak of human happiness." But Goethe has something to add: to observe nature, he says, requires a certain inner serenity that will not allow irrelevant things to disturb it.

I sense that my companion possesses some of this serenity and recall that in earlier years I was also able to dismiss irrelevant things when I reached the mountains or the sea —when I experienced the sensuality of a spring pasture swelling with growth or the clearness of a strong September gale. I am not able to do it in the same way nowadays, it and I am not sure that what is distracting me is irrelevant. Yesterday I smiled at something that has again become a reality in the light of today. In some way it is also connected with nature as I sense it now.

Of course, I still have this marvelous feeling of liberation, of experiencing something essential, perhaps simply of *living,* as I roam over an expanse affording a panoramic view of mountains in all shades of blue. It is good to walk here as father and son together, to look and listen together, to exchange a few words or keep silent together. And to have this rare feeling, all at the same time, of sensing both something new and something one has experienced before.

Basically, I suppose, we all carry within ourselves strong reminiscences of our long existence in nature. From the time man first took shape—for thirty thousand generations or more—he remained a hunter. He has tilled the soil and lived in villages for only three hundred generations, and as recently as thirty generations ago our Western European ancestors were still living in what we people of today call barbarism. Thus the life of the hunter was man's form of existence a hundred times longer than his life as a farmer or as a city-dweller.

Our history books habitually begin with man's taking

up permanent residence somewhere. This takes us back a mere ten thousand years or so, to the moment when man began tilling the soil, forming permanent communities, and founding what we like to call "civilization." But all civilization has common roots in the prehistoric past—covering a span of time a hundred times longer than history—when man was a freely roaming hunter.

It is much the same with us. Just as we have retained the biological stature of the hunter, so we carry deep within ourselves, albeit unconsciously, much of his emotional life. The hunter needs wide expanses and elbowroom: forests and waters, savannas and mountains. He lives like the animals he hunts, within the framework of his physical environment, and he becomes part of it. He enters nature and nature enters him.

Over some hundreds of thousands of years this must have left deep marks on his emotional life, more or less strongly influencing our own experience and need of nature, no matter to what degree the outward trappings of civilization may sometimes appear to have removed us from nature. Some of this attraction toward one's origin, rudimentary and pathetically shrunk, must be what one finds at camping sites with their paltry substitutes for real nature, among the jam-packed sun worshippers of the bathing beaches, and among the demure Sunday strollers in city parks. And the intensity of our emotions as we stand in untouched or relatively untouched nature—out in open space—is probably explained by our sense of being a bit closer to our own origin.

The Persians gave us the word "paradise" which originally meant hunting ground. The American Indian dreamt of a hereafter in the "happy hunting grounds." Such visions of paradise in terms of the good hunting to be had there surely goes back to ancient habits of mind. And in our age of status thinking one of the highest measures of a man's social position is, ironically, his having a domain in which to move

, about freely, his being able to bring home fresh game or to hang an animal pelt over the shoulders of his woman—things that were the essential conditions of existence for our primitive forebears.

The hunter's life, in the deepest sense, was a life of struggle—basically, the hunt-or-be-hunted struggle for food. Hunting for animals that were often larger or faster than man required cooperation—group work. Downing a rhinoceros or a mammoth, a saber-toothed tiger or a cave bear, with primitive weapons was not to be attempted by a man alone. The pack, the flock, remained the primary social organism during the whole hunting period—as it still is among most primates and humanity's surviving "living fossils." The hunting pack was the earliest form of human organization.

It is possible with the aid of our imagination to visualize how such packs one day extended their forays out from the East African central plateau which first saw man emerge. There must have been some connection between this exodus and the violent climatic changes that accompanied the periodic advances and retreats of the great ice masses and caused steppes and tropical rain forests, tundras, needle forests, and deserts to be shifted from one place to another. Perhaps curiosity about the unknown was a contributing incentive.

Because of an enormous amount of water locked within the wandering cloak of ice, the sea level is low. Over the Nile country, across the land bridges that once divided the Mediterranean into three inland seas, bands of hunters are migrating toward the virgin hunting grounds of the Eurasian land mass. Moving overland, some small groups of hunters reach southern England and Indonesia. Taking thousands of generations, this continuing migration goes on at a very slow pace. But some five hundred thousand years before our hydrogen bomb, the fires of the hunter are burning in caves and camps from the Atlantic to the western coast of the Pacific.

In addition to his primitive weapons, man creates the axe, and for a quarter of a million years it remains his principal tool, developing from a coarse, barely shaped stone into a definite shape. The axe tells a fascinating story, for wherever it is found, from the Atlantic to the Cape and the Indus, it is basically of the same design. Such uniformity would have been impossible, surely, unless many of the groups had had some contact with each other.

Let the imagination play with the fact of the stone axe. When different hunting packs meet in each other's territories, the encounters probably result in violence most of the time. The stranger is fair game, after all, much as the beasts of the forest are, and moreover, his presence is a threat to the food resources of one's own flock. But sometimes, perhaps, there is a need to make contact with a neighboring group. A messenger signals his peaceful errand by some special sound or face paint—an early version of the flag of truce—and a kind of primitive diplomacy develops. In time certain neighboring groups agree to live in a state of armed neutrality, in a kind of elementary coexistence. Such contacts give rise to the first beginnings of a common culture. It may take generations before a new invention is spread to a larger area, but the hunting age has plenty of time. The axes demonstrate that the constantly moving groups of hunters created something akin to a human community in embryo.

But there are also forces working in the opposite direction. The groups are still small, and they are often widely separated. Some of them have penetrated mountain passes and reached areas into which others do not follow. Moreover, nature creates new dividing lines: as the ice melts and the sea level rises, large areas of land are cut off from their mother continents. Geographical expansion breeds isolation,

isolation breeds genetic distinctions. Different racial patterns begin to take shape.

Homo sapiens thus splits into different races. Over a very long period of time, differing species of erect primates have met, imparted the culture of the stone axe to each other, competed for hunting territory, fought one another. As the ice recedes to the south for the last time, Homo sapiens is left alone on the stage. He has overwhelmed the other species of the genus Homo, here and there perhaps also mixing his blood with theirs and thereby broadening his genetic base.

With Homo sapiens the hunting age moves toward its culmination. At the same time, frequent changes in climate are creating new barriers that will help to shatter the homogeneity of the axe culture. Drier weather transforms the interior of the rich hunting grounds of the Sahara into a vast desert. Like most of East Asia, Africa south of the desert —this Africa which saw man emerge, placed the first tool in his hand, and probably also gave him the stone axe—is cut off from the mainstream of development, and the southern part of Eurasia, with an offshoot into the Africa of the Nile, becomes the heartland of the creative changes that are now occurring—changes that will be of decisive importance for the future of man.

These changes are tied first and foremost to flint—a substance that has meant immeasurably more in man's development than gold. Long before there were roads for dealers in amber and silk, there were trading routes for flint, a hard but easily worked stone that enabled the hunter to enlarge and improve his arsenal of weapons and tools. With flint tools he can make better use of the hide and bones of game he has killed. From a split fragment of bone he makes the needle his most important invention since the axe a quarter of a million years earlier—with which he can make better clothing from animal pelts. The needle also makes it possible for him to join pelts into tents and thus to move from caves and rock crevices out into the open. Fire and the needle allow man to retain some of the temperate climate close to his own body even in frosty areas. The products of the needle, clothes and tents, widen his living space.

He invents the bow and arrow, thereby multiplying the length and strength of his arm. He tames the wolf—the first animal to be made subject to man's will—and it becomes the dog, the hunting companion. Man, bow, dog—they become the trinity of the advanced hunting age.

Still, large virgin lands are waiting. As the ice retreats for the last time, it leaves room for an abundant animal life in northern Eurasia. There the mammoth, weighed down with flesh, sounds his trumpet. There the reindeer skulk, the moose amble, wild boars root, wild horses thunder—and with his needle and his fire the hunter is able to follow such game all the way to the receding ice line.

A band of hardy hunters crosses the dry land of Bering sound to Alaska. A new continent has been discovered, with hunting grounds that must appear happy, even to the living. Fire, bow, and needle are carried along by the emigrants as they spread southward along the Rocky Mountains and on to prairies swarming with buffalo, down to the high valleys of the Andes, down to the Amazon Delta and Tierra del Fuego. Here is the cultural legacy of the Old World on which the Inca and Maya peoples, and the Aztecs and Toltecs, will build their cultures—the legacy of a world from which the immigrants are to be separated for several millennia when the ocean comes pressing on again, washing out the bridge between the hemispheres.

By the time the ice has receded to a circle around the turning point of the globe, man the hunter has spread over all continents. In scattered flocks he ranges over Eurasia and on the twin American continents. In primitive craft he has reached even Australia and Tasmania. In the original African land his hunting call is still heard, as it was a million years ago. Earth has been conquered by man.

The world conquered by the hunter is one of enormous expanses and large distances. Distances have split the community of man into many parts but they retain a common base. The pattern of the hunter's life is much the same everywhere. He lives in a pact with nature—on the plains, under the stars. Nature determines the rhythm of his day and his years, filling him with impressions, creating the framework of his emotional experiences.

Some of this must still be present deep within two mountain hikers, as they take in the broad vista at the entrance of Utla valley, as it widens into a cauldron of green and rust, while the crests of Skogadalsnosi and Hillerhö comb the sky, and a vestigial outcrop of the ice age, Smörstabb glacier, glitters at the rim of Gravdal peak.

The conscious part of the mind is like the visible tenth of an iceberg. Most of it is below the surface. Somewhere in this invisible portion is the wilderness of the hunter—just as in the final analysis our material civilization rests on the hunter's fire, his stone axe and flint knife, his bone needle and his bow. Nor is the road from the wilderness a long one. After all, the wilderness has been the natural environment of man for all but the last hundredth of his existence so far. It is as if a man of fifty had been a savage all his life except during the last six months.

Surely some of our deepest needs are still those of the hunter in the wilderness. The tension between these basic needs and the civilized way of life we have only recently made our own—perhaps this tension explains much of man's lessness and restlessness, his neuroses and his anxieties.

It must have been the pressure of outward necessity that led man to till the soil and take up permanent residence.

Again, the climatic shifts of the ice ages disrupted the previous order of things and thus mapped a new course for man. Earlier they had played a decisive part in the very emergence of man; later they were certainly among the rootlessness and restlessness, his neuroses and his anxieties. factors that inspired flocks of early hunters to migrate from their original continent; still later, they cut many of the groups off from each other; and finally they became the force that made man change his form of life. These climatic changes were, then, the prime instrumentality in the release of what we today call civilization.

So long as there was ample game in the forests ,the hunter had no pressing reason to change his way of life. True, his womenfolk collected and prepared the edible plants and fruits of the earth but such activity was merely a complement to the main order of the day—hunting game. However, the drier climate that followed in the wake of the last ice age must have shrunk the forests and made the wilderness poorer in game over wide areas—in the Iranian highlands, on the slopes of the Andes. And in just such areas man had to find new sources of food or else perish. He met the challenge by making what had been a supplementary activity his main industry. At about the same time he started domesticating his animal food. The era called the Neolithic, the style of which even now dominates the greater part of mankind, began to take shape.

Thus, man began to cultivate grainbearing grasses and to bring under the will and sway of his brain the wild sheep, goats, cows, and boars that roamed the highlands. It was a gradual development, but by comparison with the lengthy hunting age the transformation was revolutionary in its speed. Once the new style of life had spread from the high plateaus of Iran to the rich mudlands of the Mesopotamian twin-river country, and somewhat later to the basins of the Nile and the Indus rivers, the foundation was laid for a development that would lead to Shakespeare, the United Nations, and the space rocket. All that we call culture or civilization is after all, as somebody has aptly put it, nothing but a second flowering of barley, wheat, and rice.

For man the permanent resident caves and tents were no proper home. Mud huts, forerunners of the Tower of Babel and the Empire State Building, were built, and soon there were groups of huts clustered together in primitive agricultural villages. Some of the villages grew into cities, some cities into states, some states into empires.

Throughout the long age of hunters the primary biological and social unit had been the flock, and the earliest clay houses were clearly intended to be cohabitations for entire clans. Village existence gradually changed all this, however, for it led to a marked division of clans into families while simultaneously creating much larger communities and thus providing the basis for a division of labor hitherto unknown. In hunting, everyone's full attention had been concentrated on capturing the food—food that was, after all, so mobile that finding and killing it was a full-time job. Agriculture and living in settled villages, on the other hand, created the conditions in which specialized trades—metallurgy, commerce, literature—could develop.

Men of the age of hunting had practiced a kind of primitive communism, in which all and sundry cooperated in the search for food. The strongest, the most intelligent, or the most daring emerged as natural leaders, the food and booty acquired under their leadership was shared by all in the pack. Village life introduced a new scale of social values—one involving possessions and even opulence. It institutionalized acquired and inherited prosperity, eventually giving rise to class struggles and billionaires—and to the collecting of the things that may prompt a hiker in the mountains, carrying only the bare necessities in his rucksack, to think of many civilized homes as genteel junk closets and

95

of a great deal that we call luxury as gilded poverty.

Stationary existence also institutionalized war. The roots of war cut deep through human existence, indeed, all the way through to the prehuman quick. But the battles of hunting bands that came upon each other in the forest had been part of an elemental struggle for existence, scarcely different from the hunt for other animals. Just as the hunter killed his game, so he fought—and often killed—his competitors for that game. When hunting ceased to be the main industry, this pattern persisted in the mud hut villages—but with one major change. The scope of the old territorial struggle was widened. Village life transformed war into a social institution.

As villages became more prosperous, their riches became all the more of a temptation to wandering bands of herdsmen and hunters—and of course one's village had to be defended against such marauders. At the same time, a growing town could become all the more prosperous as it widened its base for raw materials by the obvious means of raiding weaker tribes and forcing other peoples to pay tribute. Thus the resident and the nomad became natural enemies. Cain, the tiller of the soil in the rich river valley, feared Abel, the roaming herdsman and hunter, and slew him when they met in the field. Or perhaps he made him a serf: permanent settlement and war bred slavery.

Cities with accumulated wealth regarded each other with envy. The earliest historical records tell of fights among the Sumerian city-states, the Ur of Abraham and other cities along the Euphrates. These are documents of primitive savagery in the remote past, and yet they relate events that seem recognizably close to us who lived through the war of the corporal. Oftentimes the fights were over possession of the water needed by the fields—even today one is sometimes reminded that the word "rivalry" derives from the Latin *rivus*, "river." Wars also helped build the social pyramid. The city's perpetual battles against nomads and against competing cities created a need for professional soldiers, and the soldiers had to have leaders—even a "supreme" commander. Such a position gave a man power: the warlord became king, made power hereditary, founded dynasties.

Permanent settlement also led to the institutionalizing of religious ideas and their expression. The origin of such ideas, deep in the hunting age, is difficult to capture; budding ideas of forces outside man himself have left no evidence which the spade can bring to the surface. Morever, it would have been in the nature of these ideas to move in an obscurity beyond reflection and daylight. But one can surmise that they were tied to the primary elements in the existence of primitive man. Buddha himself, in his wisdom, taught that hunger and love are the origin of all human history. They must also have inspired man's religious ideas. Hunger and love—and death.

What a momentous day it must have been for primitive man when it dawned on him that his days were counted! This discovery, perhaps coupled with dreams of the dead, must have given rise in his slowly awakening mind to nebulous concepts of some kind of continuous existence after death—in other hunting grounds, or perhaps in some dismal shadow world from which the dead were to be prevented from returning to disturb the living, by bedding them down in the earth, a funeral custom practiced as early as the Neanderthal period.

Some features in the awakening world of religious ideas emerge more concretely in the animal paintings created by a prehistoric Picasso on the rock walls of certain obscure stalactite caves. Or in the Venus figures, round of bust and loins, that archaeologists have unearthed, in their obtrusive physical appearance little different from the inflated sex queens of our modern dream factories. Hunger and love, hunting and fertility, food and reproduction—these were central to the magic of primitive man. The act of depicting

97

the hunted prey or the fertile woman became a magic rite in itself—and the very rite became the reality of primitive religion.

When the hunter settled down, he brought the rites of the forest with him into the plowed field. The Egyptians gave their gods the attributes of certain animals. Man's fertility and that of the soil were identified with each other. The phallus also blessed the seed of the earth—indeed, it still raises its flowered rod in the Maypoles of today. The sun, whose life-giving strength had long been known to the hunter, became a mighty ruler over lean and fat years. Whether as a deity in itself or as an instrument of forces imagined more in the image of man, the sun required the homage of a cult—lest it decline to give forth the rich harvests needed to keep hunger at bay. Thus, the division of labor of the village turned the shaman of the hunter into the keeper of the temple—one closer than ordinary men to the sun and the stars, and a go-between to the transcendental. His close connection with the forces that had to be placated gave him predominant power close by the side of the supreme commander—with whom, indeed, he often became identical.

At some stage in all this, puzzling questions about the origin of everything began to provoke certain minds. The first of the early cosmogonies arose in response. Somewhere in the Near East a myth of creation was born, and eventually a small tribe of herdsmen from Ur, who must have borrowed the myth from the Babylonians, bequeathed it to the Occident.

It was also tempting to give memorable events of the past, as preserved and transformed by oral tradition, a mythological basis. Some of these strange accounts, such as that of the Babylonians concerning the great flood, were widely dispersed—as witness that reeling old man in his ark who is still sailing on our own sea of collected legends and songs.

Other stories were attempts to ascribe mythological significance to the peculiar characteristics of one's own tribe. Thus, the special religion of a growing, and therefore constantly threatened, community encouraged a feeling of social cohesion. One's own tribal god became a peculiar god for a peculiar people, and compared with him all other gods were abominable. The god of one's tribe promised protection against the attackers—and success in one's own attacks. He promised new promised lands when the area hitherto cultivated became barren or too small. The settled community also required sets of rules for coexistence, and since religious and political leadership were already closely interwoven (or even identical), it was quite natural for the beginnings of governance to be erected on a transcendental base.

This complex mixture of profound and trivial elements, combining the visionary and the mundane, produced the environment within which the great founders of religions and explainers of the world made their appearance. Out of the original primitive world of ideas was born the brooding over the meaning of life which, in fascinating parallels between various cultures within the span of a few centuries, allowed Isaiah and Zarathustra, Lao-tse and Confucious, Jesus and Buddha to emerge, and which also kindled the fire of the Greek intellectual adventure. It was a spiritual blast-furnace, which gave the world almost all of its large and still-viable religions, religions that would later acquire rigid and divisive outward forms and be used for purposes diametrically in opposition to the visions of their founders, but sharing nonetheless a common store of moral rules that are still the prime foundation of decent human coexistence.

It may have been no mere accident that the cradle of the great religions was southern Asia, where the heavy lines of the landscape itself seem to inspire deep meditation, and where the meeting, merging, and breaking up of various cultures must have created a distinctive soil for spiritual germination. Europe, in the meantime, was still largely on the outskirts of things. And perhaps it was no coincidence that the Asian remained the introvert when, somewhat later, a newly awakened Europe noisily took on the extroverted task of furthering man's material development on the ruins of the Bronze Age.

This westward shift in the geographic focal point of man's expansive material development was brought about by iron. Europe had iron in her bogs, and charcoal for smelting it in her forests. The age of iron became the age of Europe. With iron man could make more efficient agricultural implements—and, of course, mightier weapons. Europe received spiritual assets from the East but entered so deeply into the Iron Age as to forge even the imported creeds in iron.

The continent of iron, facing the sea with more coastal than inland area in its ragged geography, became the continent of expansion, whose sailors and soldiers would rivet distant parts of the globe together. For some thousands of years dispersed civilizations had occasionally come into contact at certain cultural crossroads in the old heartland and across the dry oceans of the Eurasian steppes, and arms, tools, ideas, and designs had been exchanged on such occasions. But it was the sailing ship, those dragon-stemmed vessels and caravelles of an outgoing, acquisitive Europe—ships built of wood from European forests, and nailed together by European iron—that made it possible to bring the continents closer to each other.

The era of great discoveries, as it is often called, was basically an age of rediscovery. Peoples who had gone their separate ways during the vast migrations of the hunting age, and then been separated by climatic and geological upheavals, were once again eye-to-eye. Diverse races, diverse though originally of the same blood, confronted each other once again—and the meeting was not a peaceful one. Just as the earlier Homo sapiens seems to have had no qualms about annihilating other erect species, so the exploration-happy and gold-thirsty conquistadors of Europe considered the inhabitants of other continents fair game. The confrontation of the continents turned into a *conquista* in blood.

The conquerors' priests form the vanguard with their blessing—rosary in one hand, sword in the other. In Montezuma's capital city, Cortés kills as many people in the name of His Highest Catholic Majesty as atomic bombs were later to sweep away at Hiroshima and Nagasaki. In the name of the Holy Trinity, Pisarro sends his cavalry charging into the defenseless Incas of Peru. In the northern half of the double continent, a white Cain meets an Abel of slightly darker hue —and a million or more freely hunting prairie Indians are exterminated to make room for a couple of hundred million whites. In the southern half, uncounted numbers of the aborigines are pauperized on the promise of paradise in another world after death, in exchange for the hell provided for them on earth. Many of the distinctive products of a high Bronze Age culture are destroyed. The enormous library of the Toltecs in Taxco is burned for the glory of God; the Maya library in Yucatan is destroyed in the same way and for the same ostensible purpose. And all too soon the sailing ships are put to still another task—in addition to their continuing one of transporting conquistadors and hidalgos to the new lands and returning to Europe laden with gold. Now there are slave ships crossing the ocean with cargoes of human beings stolen from the very continent on which humanity itself originated.

Europe, so newly uprooted from its corner on the periphery of civilization, writes a few lines of history—with iron and in blood. Peoples that had only recently been living in caves, huddling around camp fires by night and hunting by day, now disseminate themselves, their languages, their creeds, and their material culture to other continents. Puny states on the coast of Europe become world empires, and for a few fleeting centuries expansive pale-faced man behaves as if he were master of the world, and considers himself superior to any man to whom the sun gave a darker pigmentation.

All of this is so very close to us in time and yet, in a way, so distant from the secluded corner we two hikers have sought. Down there, where the Big and Little Utla valleys converge in an enormous kettle shaped by the Ice Age, three rivers meet in foam and cataracts. Brooks hang like silver tassels down the mountainsides. Around the peaks to the south, clouds are collecting in constantly changing formations, drifting in wedges like a light smoke along the valley toward the crest over Gjertvass lake. Faggots of splintered sun-rays are thrown on to the slopes through windows in the clouds. And above this landscape a sky so marvelously free—should it not be possible to attain here that inner clarity of which Goethe spoke?

But I have only to raise my hand toward the cloud-bound mountains to feel the wind from Europe—the continent with a name borrowed from the Builder of the Clouds: "the far-seeing." I think of the wind carrying the ships of Europe around the world, the wind that made Europeans the far-seeing and far-acting ones.

It was an episode, a few paltry lines in the history of man. For the wind has changed its direction—as all winds do, sooner or later. Power-happy Europe has been forced to withdraw its colonial majors and inspectors. At Lake Tanganyika, the statues of the white discoverer who first looked out over these tracts—though he had, after all, discovered nothing, having done no more than return to the cradle whence his tribe once came—are now overturned.

Even so, the consequences of the European expansion and rediscovery cannot be erased completely.

If someone from another system of stars had been able to observe Tellus five hundred years ago, he would have seen a number of isolated civilizations: in the city of Montezuma and around the Thames, in Moscow and Lahore, in the Middle Kingdom and the Land of the Rising Sun. European expansion erased these differences in part—sometimes by violently blowing up the foundations of a distinctive civilization. Our own time, with its rapid communications, is about to complete the work. Ideas and mass-produced commodities are spread over the globe with remarkable speed, on beams of light and sound or by propellers churning water and air, and encourage a global conformity of interests and expectations. The slowly developed social pattern of the Axe Age for the community of man is moving toward resurrection in a modern form.

But this leveling process is taking place in a world of bitter external contrasts, and one in which there are many vestiges of the isolation that accompanied the dispersal of the hunting groups and destroyed the axe community .The wheels of technical progress spin ever faster, touching even our neighbors in the planetary system, but they spin unevenly. From one moment to the next an astronaut launched from Cape Kennedy may pass over the bushmen of the Kalahari, with a tribal organization still based on hunting, or the Stone Age people who still dwell in the mountain caves of New Guinea, or a great and powerful modern metropolis.

Such contrasts are a reminder of how new our material civilization is, how close in time it is to the sometimes forgotten and displaced age of hunters. How short the step from prehistoric caves to the Ur of the Sumerians and Abraham, how much shorter the step from Ur to the urbs of today.

Hurtling along in his capsule, high above the paths of the eagle and the plow of wild geese, the astronaut passes over land masses that it took primitive hunting bands hundreds of millennia to occupy—and he does it in half an hour or so.

He sees no frontiers, but on the surface of the earth those manifestations of the primeval territorial instinct are still to be found. That instinct was part of the hunter as he settled down, and it led to the first city-states in the Land of the Twin Rivers. That instinct matured in the European idea of the national state, and it flowed into the master-race ideologies on which world empires were founded. That instinct has led of late to a greater splintering of space into separate states than at any time in history—while at the same time the globe has shrunk into the palpable unity which the astronaut sees below him.

These outward contrasts between the survival of archaic conditions and ideas and a sophisticated globe-circling technology, force the question: where do we find a standard, how do we achieve a synthesis? It is the worrisome question of how an incessantly growing world population, its brains increasingly glutted with dangerous knowledge, is to manage the world first conquered by the hunter on his naked feet.

Night is about to catch up with us, and we pause for a moment to take in the softening lines and evening hues of the landscape. The sun is sending the day's last few slanting rays through clouds tumbling violently around the peaks. The Builder of Clouds kneads and shapes tirelessly, creating a wreath of illusions. A torn-off rag of cloud over Skoga valley changes its shape incessantly. Camel or weasel? Now, for a few seconds, it is rolled into a little ball tossed by the wind. Like the shred off a cosmic cloud on which we are milling about making history.

Such may be the play of thoughts as you find your way through the birch brush into the valley.

6

. . . booked solid for
our trip into space . . .

WALKING IN THE MOUNTAINS, ONE CAN BE SEIZED BY A
feeling of being in the last outcropping of something vital.
Here, truly, there is elbowroom.

Elbowroom that man is about to lose. With each new
generation, it becomes harder to find. For two solitary wanderers in the pathless, it may be felt as a bit of good fortune
to belong to a generation that still has the chance to find
open space and quiet.

In a mountain valley in the home of the giants, seething
with sunshine after a gray morning, the quiet can seem almost physically palpable. It is not the mute stillness that goes
with isolation, but a stillness within which we perceive all
around us the processes of nature herself. A bird call from
the sky, the prattle of an invisible brook, a gust of wind comb-
ing the coarse mountain grass—all such things are sounds
and movements that belong to the stillness and, if anything,
serve to strengthen it.

Or, as just now a herd of wild reindeer running down a

mountain slope toward Gjertvass glacier, cloven like a fish-tail and embracing the shiny black rock with its bluish whiteness. For a while the antlers throw their silhouettes against the horizon. Then the herd runs headlong down the valley, all without making a sound. The white rumps of the females disappear behind some boulders, and the herd is devoured by the mountain. Then from somewhere comes the craw-craw of a buzzard, and you can imagine granite, gurgling glaciers, and pagan sacrifices in his call.

Even in the midst of our own time you may experience a scene like this as a fragment of something remote, much in the way that the potsherds an archaeologist digs up lend substance to his visions of past cultures. In the face of such a fragment, your imagination may play for a time on the theme of man and space.

In a world where a struggle for survival lasting over millions of years has created a kind of balance among various living beings, from the virus to the whale, from the shell to the eagle, a certain creature suddenly totters erect out of the green obscurity in the forest of his day and goes in search of food in new hunting grounds. An upstart in creation conquers and the earth and multiples and replenishes it.

His dispersion is slow during the first million years, and so is the propagation of his species. In the elemental struggle for existence man, like every other living thing, is subject to the harsh law of natural selection. To start with, tribute was exacted by the hunt for fleeing animals fighting for their own lives; that struggle filled the life of primitive man to a degree. that made him paint their images on his cave walls in a sort of obsession. The hunter has his brain and his primitive weapons; the animals he hunts have their fangs, claws, and horns. Morever, the hunting bands are dependent on their mobility, and there can have been little sentimental regard for the weak and the worn-out who are unable to help to capture food and who diminish the mobility of the flock.

The whole age of the hunter is one in which the representatives of species man are few and far between. They constitute only a small portion of the living creatures of the planet. Wide, open space is man's natural habitat.

It has been assumed that the whole population of the world, at the time when the climatic shifts of the last ice age were forcing certain tribes of hunters to settle down, amounted to some fifteen million. It was as if the present-day population of Scandinavia were dispersed over all continents on the globe—a mere ten thousand years ago.

Permanent settlement, accompanied by agriculture and the beginnings of urbanization, increased the pace of propagation—but not by much. It took another couple of thousand years for the human race to double its numbers. About four thousand years ago the Chinese took the first census of which we have knowledge. It took into account only the country that in the age of distances was to see itself as the Middle Kingdom. The population of the entire planet at this time—as long before the birth of Christ as we are now past it—was some fifty or sixty million.

In the December days of the year Zero, when Caesar Augustus decreed that the whole world would be taxed, the Roman empire alone—and for Augustus, in what was still the age of distances, the empire was the world—had as many people as the entire planet had had two thousand years before. If his decree had been obeyed to the letter, some two hundred million people would have been entered in the global population register—less than a third of the population of China today.

In the course of the next fifteen hundred years, with Europe busy rediscovering the world that had been splintered during the age of the hunter, another doubling occurred, so that early in the seventeenth century the population of the world, as estimated with a fair degree of accuracy, was well over four hundred million—an eighth of what it is today.

Now the pace quickens: in two centuries another doubling, and by the middle of the nineteenth century there are a billion or more people on earth. Europe, caught up in expansive rhythm of the Industrial Revolution, has been responsible for most of the recent growth. In the century when Europe is busily preoccupied in firming up its temporary world hegemony, the population of the continent climbs from one hundred seventy-five million to four hundred million. Thus Europe alone attains the same population as that of the entire world two hundred fifty years earlier.

The next doubling of the world population requires less than a hundred years: the two billion mark is passed shortly after 1940. In a single century man has increased his numbers as much as he had in the course of all previous history and prehistory.

But even this is only a prelude to the problem of our own time, toward which the pondering before the sherd must inevitably lead. From now on the curve soars wildly. It runs upward at a speed outdating all figures very quickly: today there are some three and a half billion of us on earth.

I am looking at my companion and reflecting that in the course of his seventeen years he has acquired a billion or so additional fellow travelers—as many newcomers as there were people on the earth barely a century ago.

By a steep ascent we have reached a small wooden shed on the Emperor peak. In the valley below Lake Gjertsvann is a green mirror between steep hillsides. It must have taken us about an hour to get up here; our watches are stowed in the rucksacks, so we can only guess.

While resting, we make a few quick calculations. Since we left the green water in the valley an hour ago, the living multitude of man has increased by seven thousand new citizens. Take a minute to catch your breath on the hill, and during that minute Tellus takes on another one hundred fifteen human passengers for its cosmic voyage—two new passengers each time the wrist-watch, that handcuff of man, ticks off a second.

On every day of the year three hundred and twenty thousand new human beings open their unsteady eyes in a steadily more crowded world, and the net increase of the world's population amounts to one hundred and sixty-five thousand individuals. It is as if a medium-sized city were populated from scratch—every day.

In the course of a year the human species increases by sixty million—by an amount equal to the entire population of the earth four thousand years ago. In a decade, another Europe is added to the world. More than that—with every passing decade the annual increment rises in geometrical progression, with interest compounded as new generations reach fertility. By the end of this century, it has been calculated, the annual increment will be over one hundred million.

Such figures, cool and clear, offer a dramatic perspective of man's brief existence on earth. They tell of a species multiplying at a steadily increasing pace from sparse little hunting bands to what has come to be called the "population explosion."

Man multiplies. Space shrinks.

You can make the mental experiment of imagining the whole world population some fifteen hundred years before the birth of Christ, when Hammurabi was setting down his laws in cuneiform and King Minos was building his labyrinth, as a mere hundred individuals, and then assuming an annual rate of population increase since then of just one percent. At that rate, the world today would now have fifteen trillion individuals. Since the dry land surface of the earth amounts to a hundred and fifty million square kilometers, there would

109

be one representative of the genus Homo for each square meter—each ten square feet—of land: in fields and forests, in deserts and swamps, in mountains and on glaciers.

Of course, the increase in population during the long primitive stage and far into what we call historic time amounted only to one or a few paltry pro mille. It was a matter of pro mille well into the present century, and it was not until about 1950 that the full percentage point was reached.

But today the rate of annual increase is no longer just the one percent of our mental experiment. It now has reached two percent—and in some parts of the world three percent and more. At that rate the population of the earth will need only thirty-five years to double itself.

By the next century mark, when my companion will have reached my present age, the population of the earth will be well over six billion, other things being equal. This is the obvious probability we have to live with—unless the poison bomb sweeps our species off the surface of Tellus before then. That mankind will have time to apply the brakes to population increase effectively before the year 2000 seems most unlikely.

That far ahead, we can see with tolerable clarity. From there on, all calculations become horrible. Redoubling ourselves once every thirty-five years, we could expect to reach the stage of one individual for every ten square feet of land in just five hundred years—a span of time less than that from Columbus to the first astronaut—a wink of the eye in the history of man. We would then have reached the point of "standing room only" on earth, and within another half century we would have not even that.

That point will not actually be reached, of course. The whole mental experiment is an absurdity. The limits of the possible are much narrower.

With an understandable bias, the experts see the population question as essentially a problem of balance between the world's population and its resources. But let the experts argue about precisely how large a population the earth can feed. Their quarrel is only one of degree, and even the most sanguine of the optimists among them are now talking in the neighborhood of fifty billion—a limit we could expect to meet, at our present rate of growth, not long after the year 2100, within a few generations. Since only half of Tellus' land surface is usable—the rest is mountains or desert, snow-covered or burnt out—a world population of fifty billion would mean that for every individual there would be only thirteen thousand square feet. Deducting space for homes, factories, communications, it would be perhaps only eight thousand square feet. Eight thousand square feet to produce all that the individual needed in the way of food, housing, clothes —a mere fraction of the space that has until now been considered the minimum. It would mean, at best, rather niggardly living conditions for mankind.

Other experts, less optimistic, contend that adequate living conditions can be created on earth for fifteen billion people at the most. At the present rate of increase, this limit would be reached sometime during the next century, in the world of our grandchildren.

Admitting that we may expect the rate of population growth to be reduced by various conditions, the fact remains that no matter how you look at it—whether your calculations are based on optimistic or pessimistic premises—man is in imminent danger of reaching a critical stage in his history, unless the curve of proliteration is turned downward very soon and very radically.

The rotating globe is about to become booked solid for our trip into space.

What has created man's dilemma is that he alone among all living creatures has repealed the law of natural selection.

We can try a few comparisons as we slowly start our

steep zig-zag ascent up toward Fanaråken ridge, while the panorama around us steadily widens. There the soft outline of one glacier sinks below us, here the glistening snow massif of another shoots ahead—and the nearest peaks seem to raise their white crests the more daringly with each upward step we take.

Consider the classic example of the microscopic amoeba. Splitting in half just once every hour it would produce sixteen million amoebas in a day and a night, and a lump as large as the earth—if there were nourishment enough—in less than a week. Or take sparrow's eggs. If all were hatched and the broods survived, the world would be oversparrowed within a few centuries. If the largest land animal were allowed to multiple unhindered in the same way, it would only take just a bit longer for the world to be overelephanted.

As for man—the basic mechanism of overpopulation is in man's having freed himself from the checks that keep other species in line. What bitter irony is in the fact that in other areas of the selective process man is the conductor and guide, limiting and sometimes exterminating wildlife, planning production and animal husbandry—all the while remaining unable to tame his own species.

The population explosion is not being caused by any sudden increase in human fertility. That factor is seemingly what it has always been. There has been a great change, however, in the balance between human fertility and death. In earlier times, fatal organic diseases and decimating epidemics kept down the rate of population increase, functioning, so to speak, as natural brakes that were built into the biological order. Up until the eighteenth century, one child in three died before reaching his first birthday, and the average life span was just a little over thirty years. But during the Industrial Revolution along the coasts of the Atlantic ocean, scientific and technical progress increased the ability of the white man to control his own environment. As his living conditions and hygiene improved, the death rate gradually declined. The net result: from 1750 to 1900 the population of Europe and North American increased by two hundred fifty percent, that of the rest of the world by less than a hundred percent.

The lessons learned gradually in the western industrial nations are now about to be applied quickly on a global scale. Thus, during the past few decades a huge campaign has been mounted in the poorer countries against malaria, yellow fever, and other scourges that used to kill hundreds of millions. The results have been quite dramatic. Our vaccines, antibiotics, and insecticides are not only effective—at least in the short·run—but inexpensive. By relatively negligible expenditures of money, hundreds of thousands of people can be spared premature death. The decline in the death rate that it took Europe a couple of centuries to accomplish has been achieved within just a few years in some of the underdeveloped countries—and this, moreover, at a much earlier stage of social and economic development, before conditions for a better life have been created.

Man seems on the verge of attaining what almost amounts to death control. Unfortunately, he has not combined this with birth control. He is removing the natural brakes that hitherto kept population growth within bounds, but he has not been able—or he has not chosen—to replace those natural brakes with workable artificial ones.

The consequences of man's eliminating the machinery of natural selection are twofold. For one thing, owing to improvements in hygiene and medicine, biological defects that used to be weeded out of the human species in its struggle for survival are now being passed along from generation to generation. Biologists have already been able to trace a certain progressive deterioration of the species as a result of this. There is of course nothing to do but to take note of the fact; social conscience having been awakened, there is no going back to the haphazard and mericiless weeding of times past.

The second consequence, even more menacing in the short run, is causing the greatest alarm among the experts. Science and technology have not been able to increase world food production enough to meet the needs of the soaring world population. Mass death has been fought successfully by medical science, with the ironic result that mass dearth is on the increase. Modern medicine and hygiene save hundreds of thousands of human lives every year—only to surrender them to starvation. The cool calorie tables of the statisticians tell us of the ever-increasing numbers of people who are seriously and chronically undernourished, not only in absolute figures but also in relative proportions. As the tent of night moves across the globe this evening, two thirds of humanity are going to their rest with hungry bellies.

The realm of hunger is already the largest of realms, and it grows larger every day, without let up.

All this we know. International agencies and mass media are spraying us with facts about the population explosion that lays claim to more than the world has power to produce. But it is as though we received the bad news, which has come to us in a rush, only in the abstract. As though imagination boggled at taking to heart the threat to life our children and grandchildren may be facing.

Well over a hundred and fifty years ago, in opposition to a prevailing blind faith in a future of unbroken and unending human progress, the gentle English clergyman Thomas Malthus propounded the pessimistic notion that the prosperity of the masses can never rise appreciably, since population tends always to increase faster than food supplies. His theory had principal reference to the industrial society of Great Britain, and there it did not hold good. But if Malthus were living today, he would be able to reformulate his theory

114

in global terms—and today's neo-Malthusians, no more optimistic than their master, are predicting that there will of course never be more people than there is food for, but surely not any fewer either. Left to himself, that is, man is going to multiply to the very limit of the existing resources. No spontaneous process is going to check this development. Thus, the final regulation of world population will be achieved by starvation.

In the same way, Karl Marx's accumulation theory is being dusted off. Marx held that ever larger amounts of capital would accumulate in the hands of a small number of producers. This would increasingly widen the gap between exploiters and exploited and lead, in turn, to a steady exacerbation of the class struggle. Social evolution within individual Western industrial societies has refuted the learned sociologist, but on a global scale, which Marx did not foresee, there are striking proofs for his theory in evidence today. The gap between "have" and "have-not" countries is increasing with every passing decade, notwithstanding international aid measures—and the picture is not improved by the existence in some have-not countries of a small class of super-rich people luxuriating on top of a massive foundation of poverty. Today, a third of the world's people consume three fourths of the world's food in calories. The proud ambition of the have countries is to double their standard of living in the course of a couple of decades, while in the have-not countries real income grows by only a dollar or two per year and the basis of nourishment per capita actually declines.

These theories, as formulated by Malthus and Marx, are certainly not to be accepted as blind laws of nature. Their final validity has yet to be tested. But in a strange way they do seem to converge in the situation facing mankind today. Unchecked population growth does prevent poorer countries from forming the capital that would permit a rise in the level of material existence. Conversely, it has not been possible so far to reduce the birth rate anywhere until a certain economic and cultural standard has been reached. This is a truly vicious circle—the intertwined vicious circles of Malthusianism and Marxism. Overpopulation causes starvation, and starvation causes overpopulation. The poor become more numerous and poorer. The rich, relatively speaking, fewer and richer.

This also has something to do with space. The world's people have always been unevenly distributed—in the first instance largely because of climatic conditions. This unevenness has become a prominent feature in today's population picture. Tightly packed areas exist side by side with sparsely filled or almost empty ones. Seven tenths of the world's people live on only a hundredth of its dry surface, and fully half of that space is occupied by only one tenth of the population. The growing multitudes of mankind have packed themselves together in the choicest areas on the surface of the earth, but these areas can no longer come even close to feeding all the people.

The unevenness is bound to increase even more dramatically. At mid-twentieth century, two thirds of the world population lived in the economically least developed regions; by the end of the century the figure is expected to be closer to fourth fifths. China alone, growing at the rate of some sixteen million people per annum, will have a population almost equal to that of the whole world in 1900.

Have we who skim the cream of the earth's resources even begun to realize the significance of all this?

The white race exploded and hurled itself all over the globe in a few unruly centuries of colonization and industrialization. Today it is a shrinking minority. It has been said that the white man is on his way to becoming a biological rarity—an exaggeration, of course, but perhaps not much of one. Along with this racial shift, the borderline between growing hungry nations and sparsely populated well-fed ones is increasingly a racial borderline between colored and colorless.

Can we seriously imagine for even a moment that this will not have the most far-reaching consequences?

For a long time, hunger was such a commonplace occurrence in the poor countries that it ignored its own existence. Today the hungering millions are able for the first time in history to compare their lot with that of the more privileged peoples. And conscious hunger is dynamite. Poverty becomes unbearable when it is combined with the daily opportunity of comparing itself with the affluence of others.

A starving world is simply not going to allow a class of privileged nations to remain forever in undisturbed possession. Even now we can see the front lines forming, we can perceive the outlines of a global class struggle. The have countries' programs for development and aid are no longer going to satisfy the have-nots' impatience. The West will soon be faced with demands that will, if met, fundamentally affect its own standards of living.

And those demands will certainly not stop at a more equitable distribution of the world's food and the material standards created by technology. For the masses in the portions of the globe where population pressure is greatest, space itself will probably loom as an ever more important ingredient in the living standard they want for themselves. Sparsely populated regions will exercise an irresistible attraction on the overpopulated ones, like the suction of a partial vacuum.

Malthus spoke of the man born in an overpopulated country as being "redundant" in the community. For him, as Malthus put it, there is no place at the great feast of nature. But who in the world of tomorrow will passively accept being adjudged redundant merely by virtue of his having been born in an overpopulated country? So long as the supposedly redundant suspect that there may be a bit of room for them farther down the table, they are likely to make every possible effort to elbow their way there. It would be contrary to man's biological nature for him to resign himself to the smothering death of overpopulation while his neighbor still had space and food.

In earlier days the pressure of growing population set masses on the move. It drove Attila and his Huns, Jenghis Khan, and Tamerlane from the Mongol steppes toward China, the Near East, and Europe, chasing other tribes from their pasture lands in the course of migrations that trampled the culture of antiquity under foot. When Europe exploded, in turn, a few hundred million whites acquired space in other continents at the expense of a few million people of darker pigmentation—exporting a man weighing a hundred sixty pounds cost less than importing the hundreds of tons of food he would need in a lifetime.

Today the globe may appear to be neatly staked out and divided up. But even less than yesterday's world is the world of tomorrow likely to recognize any eminent domain for tribes that once took possession of sparsely populated areas. Whether we calculate the planet's capacity to house and feed people at fifteen billion or at fifty billion, our tacit premise is a reasonably uniform distribution of these masses over the habitable portions of the earth. In a world where overpopulation increases the pressure incessantly, the haphazard barriers of national frontiers will probably come to be considered an absurdity.

Is it not possible even now to see the next turn of the tidal wave of history that has carried the white race ahead? Can we not see how long-cherished white ideas of being a master race, at the very moment that such ideas are being abandoned by the whites themselves, are now being turned against them in a new and inverted racism? To people living in crowded and desperate countries, must it not seem quite proper, and eminently practical as official policy, to visit the real and imagined past iniquities of the white man upon his children unto the third and fourth generations?

And how is our own navigation being adapted to these changing currents? Are we at all able to renounce voluntarily the preferred treatment we have long unwittingly claimed, so far as access to the good things of the world is concerned? If a shrinking white minority tries a rear-guard action to defend its privileges—its material wealth, its food calories, its space—will this not involve the risk of turning the entire planet into a kind of South Africa? Are we about to witness the very same drama, but now unfolding in reverse, that was first staged when expanding and soil-hungry whites began taking possession of land inhabited by people of darker hues? Is it now the turn of the paleface to become the last of the Mohicans?

Our own generation can do no more than pose these bothersome questions. The next generation may know the answers.

Yet the racial aspect of the population explosion, though perhaps of importance to some because it touches on the foundations of European civilization, is only a rather minor detail in the historic drama of the rise and fall of cultures, and of migrations and the spread of races. The truly significant fact is that the rising wave of population raises serious questions about the manner in which the entire human species will exist in the future.

Today, the poisonous nuclear mushroom looms as the greatest single threat to that future. If all the nuclear trigger fingers are held in check, overpopulation may well become an even more tangible threat to a coming generation. While an effective atomic war might mean an end in horror, permanent overpopulation bordering on starvation could mean a horror without end—constant crises, social convulsions, global anarchy. Or perhaps it could also harbor within itself the force that would eventually put an end to the horror.

Old premonitions in a new guise. Even in the seventeenth century the link between overpopulation and war preoccupied a number of thinkers. Linnaeus placidly declared that he was "inclined to believe that, because of some natural law, wars erupt where there is the greatest surplus of people." Thomas Hobbes, an adversary of Aristotle and a precursor of Darwin, thought not only that overpopulation was the principal cause of war, but also that it might cause the war that would end all wars by putting an end to the world. The theme is a familiar one—but today it has become topical in a dimension far beyond the ideas of the seventeenth-century thinkers.

With the jam-packed destitution of today etching its picture into the retina, can we seriously imagine there being room for decent human coexistence in a world even more crowded than the one we now inhabit? Governments founded on the ideas of democracy but incapable of satisfying the elementary needs of the starving masses have a poor chance of surviving for long. Sooner or later, overcrowding and starvation are likely to breed regimes founded on terror, with new Attilas and Jenghis Khans riding in their van. The primitive battle for territories may soon be resumed in new forms.

Thus, the twin threats of overpopulation and refined instruments of destruction may simply merge. It may be that real disarmament cannot be brought about unless the population problem is also effectively resolved. Those threatened with being smothered are likely to be tempted to use armed might in an attempt to acquire—by blackmail or direct action —what others will not cede voluntarily; to those thus threatened, or fearful of being threatened, possession of armed might for defense may appear to be a necessity. We could reach the point at which this regime or that elected in cold blood to solve its problems by the simple expedient of mass extermination of other nations, or even the point at which a government, with desperate equanimity, allowed its own population to be decimated in order to gain a temporary breathing space in a seemingly impossible situation. Thus the population bomb inside the shell of starvation could well become a military threat comparable in scope to nuclear weapons; and in a war of all against all for the limited resources and space of the globe, the population bomb could directly trigger the hydrogen bomb.

Was this where the path was to lead for the two-legged creature who usurped power over the forces of nature and spurned her laws?

Nightmares—in this stillness!

In front of me is a young man whose future means much to me. A while ago, down on the Emperor Rock, we were talking about proliferation and the law of selection. Here he is otherwise preoccupied, for at this level it is easy to be amazed by the plants that valiantly insist on their right to exist at the edge of the snow ledges of high mountains. Sturdy qualities are needed to hold one's own in an environment so inhospitable to living creatures as this one is. One has to admire these aristocrats of the high mountains, with their harmoniously balanced structure and sober glacial beauty— the Saussurea with her coquettish bows and her faint scent of vanilla, the fine brushlike flowers of the flea lane, to which the Norwegians have given the apposite name "star of the snowy slope," the ice ranunculus, which often climbs all the way to the peaks.

And this solitary mountain anemone. I still remember my father handing me, with a certain solemnity, a previous contribution to my first herbarium—a mountain anemone that he had kept for years between the covers of one of his

121

favorite books. Its dead, downy beauty awakened a longing for something beyond the forest nearby. Now, almost as a rite, my companion leans over to examine the living beauty with the care it deserves.

And then there are the big, bold lines in play wherever you look. The Skagadöl crest skewering the clouds on its peaks. The home of the giants opening its door wide toward Big Boy and Bygdin peaks. The goal of our hike on the Fanaråken ridge, which we know we are approaching, though it is not yet in sight.

Fanaråken—the mountain of my dreams ever since I first climbed it as a young man and was almost lost in a treacherous glacier crack during a lonely descent in fog. Nowhere in the Scandinavian mountains do I find a view so breathtakingly beautiful as that from the crest of Fanaråken. For my companion it is a new experience, and I am somewhat curious to see whether he will be spellbound in the same way.

And the future beyond Fanaråken? Of this I cannot know much. After all, I do not believe in any inevitable fate toward which we blindly move in our preordained parts, as in a Greek tragedy.

But isn't it enough that disaster in one form or another cannot be excluded from the possibilities looming in man's future? It would be frivolous to dismiss our nightmares with the bland assumption that somehow "everything will come out all right." The threat is there, like the writing on the wall at the feast of Belshazzar. Unless mankind is quick to limit its own growth methodically and radically, unless the abolished natural brakes are replaced by artificial ones, we are running the risk, to say the least, of reaching a denouement that may meet all reasonable requirements for classical tragedy.

The problem is that simple. Yet the solution is apparently very difficult. The obstacles continue to be numerous. The most flimsy excuse is of course the economic one: it would cost too much. The riposte is painfully self-evident: in monetary terms, how many contraceptive pills to one intercontinental ballistic missile? A generation that blithely spends trillions to increase the destructive power of its weapons, to shoot armadas of satellites around the globe, and to go to the moon where there is little for us to gain, cannot claim to lack money enough to tackle the most momentous problem confronting our whole species. The one thing we can't afford is to let things go on as they have been.

No, the economic costs are not what prevents our getting to the root of the problem. The real obstacles are the indifference that mass hunger breeds; widespread ignorance that proves to be the more difficult to overcome the more the collectives swell; and a varied assortment of ingrained habits, patterns, and prejudices. So far, when the question has been brought up in the international councils that must hammer out a solution, the response has been hushed voices and embarrassed whispers.

It has to be admitted that a few cracks have appeared in the walls of indifference, ignorance, and embarrassment. The United Nations and its organs are at least permitted to map the problem. An increasing number of overcrowded countries have made family planning a part of their national policy—though without discernible results so far except in Japan, that unique part of Asia which has adopted Western technology and culture but kept the habit of restraint acquired during four harsh feudal centuries, when the shotguns, knowing the limited resources of the country, pegged the maximum population at twenty-five million and hung the threat of severe penalties over any family that dared to breed more than the permitted number of children. Today, the realities of the population explosion are beginning to be mentioned even in the Vatican.

Are these signs of awakening?

Perhaps. And yet we are still far from having a real

population policy. Poverty, ignorance, and prejudice may well make dealing with the population crisis even harder than with the armament question, considered of itself. Military disarmament, after all, is a matter between nations, whereas dealing with the population crisis, which involves so many deeply ingrained personal habits and living patterns, necessarily requires the active cooperation of the individual. Knowing how difficult it has been to touch even the fringes of the disarmament problem, we can entertain no easy optimism about the prospect of effectively limiting population growth in the near future. And the time factor is an especially worrisome aspect of the problem. It hardly favors a solution, because the larger the masses in misery, the more difficult it becomes to awaken the individual's sense of responsibility and self-discipline.

Nightmares or not, this much we can foresee: for the next generation, the population explosion will be the most tangible of realities—the backdrop against which all other dramas will be played. This much we can imagine: it will more severely test the ability of the human race to adapt itself to changed conditions than ever before.

We approach the nearest part of Fanaråken and see the hut on the crest at a distance. A gray cloud sweeps rapidly along the slope and wraps us in a sudden thick snowfall, and we don't see the hut again until we are close by. But then the cloud is gone, as suddenly as it came. We tread a carpet of soft, sunlit new snow. The air is soft as silk, yet strong.

Again on Fanaråken, again this view. Over the fan-shaped massifs of Horung and Skagadöl peaks a fascinating play unfolds, with clusters of clouds and mountain peaks as the actors, and with sun windows permitting the great master of lighting to throw large patches of wandering light on the stage. A mystery play of nature, with scenes changing from one minute to the next. To the southwest we are looking into the deep blue of Sognefjord.

I throw a furtive glance at my companion. Oh yes, it had its effect. Fanaråken can also become a legacy.

A while on earth, a while in the large expanse—so exhilaratingly restful and free in its panoramic view. Here there is still room, as in the ages before man began his conquest of the earth.

For how long?

In the final analysis, the worst consequence of the overpopulation that threatens us is that stillness and quiet will disappear. Until now, the problem of the unbridled proliferation of the human race has been seen in terms of shortage of food. This is what has been closest by—the most immediate threat. But even if we could make enough bread from stone to feed billions and ever new billions of stomachs, the population crisis would still be with us.

For the most vital question, in the end, is not simply how many stomachs the earth can feed, but how mankind is going to live—the quality of life. It is a question having to do with man's deepest needs and with his balance with nature. No matter what technical progress the human brain may achieve, something essential is certain to be lost as ever-larger masses of people are packed together in settlement areas covering ever-larger portions of the globe. A society of human termites is not so far distant—indeed, the first nests have already been built, giving us a foretaste of the choking, smothering atmosphere in which future men will live unless the brakes are applied, and soon.

Towards evening, with the mercury a few degrees below freezing, new snow clouds come drifting in. We spend the night in the hut at the crest. At dawn we tie ourselves together with ropes and walk across the glacier to the north. Fanaråken disappears in the clouds behind us.

The sea is waiting.

7

". . . plunderers of
our own nest . . ."

TWILIGHT STRIKES A BLUE CHORD BETWEEN SKY AND
sea. It is one of those moments when everything seems at
once tangibly near and yet floating and volatile.

We are in the archipelago west of Sweden, and from
outside Koster Island the heavy beat of waves against cliffs
and rocks can be heard. Their sound reaches us as stertorous
breathing. We ourselves are in a sheltered cove on the inside
of the island, where the water is only a light froth around
the *Thalatta,* swinging slowly and almost weightlessly on her
anchor line.

We feel pleasantly turned about. The change from mountain to sea was sudden. Throughout the day we had hard
going through the Oslo fjord. The wind was howling from
west-sou'west, and the whole of the Skagerrak pressed on
through the mouth of the fjord. The *Thalatta* rode hard into
grey-green breakers, pitching and tossing. Sometimes she
raised her stem like a wall in front of us, when a good wave
came rushing and dashed buckets of water over windshield

and canvas cover. The next second she was diving so deep into a trough that the propeller was beating empty air. It gave us a start, sometimes, when the planking went from creak to crash, and I swore at myself more than once for not having brought my companion and the *Thalatta* into snug harbor at Hanko, or at least somewhere in the Leira It was only out of foolhardy stubbornness that we chose to fight the gale.

Well, perhaps something else as well: there must have been a vague fascination with the danger of the thing, tempting us to continue on. And lying here now, in our sheltered cove, we feel a kind of satisfaction in not having avoided the ordeal.

Man and the sea, fear and temptation. We can sit snug in our cabin and recall the Greek sage who declared that there are three kinds of people—the living, the dead, and those who go to sea. With today's experience still rolling inside us, we can joke about belonging, though quite amateurishly, in the third category.

We can also indulge in a bit of fantasy about man's links to the sea. The coast dweller, whose eyes and ears have been exposed to the impact of the sea from his early years, must feel the rustle of the ground swell even when he transplants himself to another environment. For the landlubber the experience of the sea is less immediate, but even in him a dormant amphibian instinct seems to awaken as he meets it—in a hazy dawn when sky and water merge into one, in a day of strength when the fjord is streaked with white, in the serene hour of a becalmed evening.

The sea's impact on us is surely more than an esthetic impression of open horizons or the play of light over a living expanse of water. It must delve much deeper, into some obscure longing for the ocean, into an instinctive recognition. From "dust thou art" come—but ultimately from sea water. No matter how far we move away from the ocean, we always carry something of it within us. The salt of the ocean in our blood, our sweat, our tears. The lime-white building substance of the ocean in our skeleton—just as it is in the bones of fish and the shells of conchs. The protoplasm in my flesh is the same as that of the first one-cell organism in the primordial sea. Just as all life began in the sea, so my own highly temporary existence began in a miniature ocean of foetal fluid.

Somewhere, unreachably far down in the original brain, there must still be something of the rolling swell of the Devonian sea. Perhaps my own rhythmic change between sleep and wakefulness has been inherited from certain cold-blooded amphibians who lost consciousness when the chill of night swept overland, once they had left the temperate chambers of the sea. Perhaps ebb and flood tide are preserved somehow in my heart and skull. You get no further than a number of perhapses, you can only guess that there must be a deeper connection between ourselves and the brew from which life first emerged long ago—something that occurs to me, for want of a better headline, as the remnant, preserved through the ages, of an early biological mother fixation. On a hidden level, then, we all belong to that third category of people.

So one may muse, sitting in the twilight while the *Thalatta* tugs gently at her anchor line and friendly little wavelets pat her hull. "Thalatta, thalatta"—the sea, the sea! That was the cry of Xenophon's beaten, thirsty, and exhausted ten thousand when they caught their first glittering glimpse of the Mediterranean over the rim of the desert. There is a longing for the sea in the word itself, we have told ourselves; and we also like to recall that the Hellenes themselves took the word—thalatta, thalatta—from the original people they subdued. When the Hellenes first came down to the peninsula as primitive nomads from the steppes to the north, they —the people who in the Odyssey would give the world its canticle of fear and love of the blue element—had no word of their own for the sea. With what trembling and curiosity they must have gazed at the free horizon opening itself to their eyes! But I also imagine that there was an instinctive recognition as they met the line of waves after thousands of years on the steppes.

In any case, the reunion with the sea made the nomad a seafarer. In their mythology, the Hellenes had Prometheus give men not only fire but also the vessel that would carry them over the waves. As Aeschylus put it:

And the chariots of the sea, rushing forth
On wings of linen were shaped by me

As we get the *Thalatta* ready for night, we send a grateful thought to the defiant one who was fettered by the gods. A real boat—it must be of wood, not mute plastic—feels somehow alive. It plays a tune with the water and there are tones and echoes in its planking.

Before turning in we sit aft for awhile, listening to the breathing of the sea. On land, the wind stirs silhouettes of yew and hardy little pine trees. The Koster islands have retained a good deal of their original foliage, but farther down the archipelago we will meet several clean-shaven ones. On the outermost islets sea and wind have ground and shaped and smoothed; farther inshore the axe has done the work.

During the time of the Vikings, a Norse bard could speak of the Vik side, where we are now, as "the land yonder east, overgrown with oak." Now the memory of that vegetation survives only in a number of place names—like Öckerö, where the last oak bit the dust long ago. The islands' oak became ship planks and herring kegs, and where the trees had been felled, the soil lay open to the winds. When Linnaeus met the sea in amazement and "botanized on the sea-bottom as in a new Sweden," he was at the same time overcome with melancholy at the lack of forestation. He found "the whole area nude, although in ancient times forest had covered all mountains." "It is incredible," he wrote, "what difference it imparts to a land when its slopes, bereft of trees; become naked rocks, which make it appear as if it had risen a few years ago from the abyss of the sea." He declared that people ought to come here "from the wooded provinces of the realm, to see what a privilege it is to own one's own forest."

In a Scandinavian archipelago, the keen-eyed royal physician from Uppsala had caught a glimpse of an industry at which man has worked for some thousands of years, but of which the full consequences are only now beginning to dawn on us as we witness, in horror, the destruction of the environment that forms the very basis of our existence. Those clean-shaven islands that so frightened Linnaeus are, after all, nothing but innocent idylls compared to the ruins man has left in his wake along the main roads of history.

Only the merest glimpses of man's history have been written down on clay tablets or parchment scrolls. Human history loses its thread unless the relationship between man and his natural environment is kept in mind. Real history is written in the ground: in the marshes where Babylon once dazzled with its splendor, in the sand dunes now covering the palaces and brothels of Carthage, in fleeced hillsides that once carried hanging gardens, in muck-filled rivers and emptied lakes. The mightiest ruins on man's road are not those we meet on the Acropolis or the Roman Forum. They are ruined landscapes.

This industry, like so much else, was started when man began tilling the soil. During the whole of his primitive existence man, like the other animals, had lived in balance with his environment. Where he sought his prey, the hunter wrought less change than the beaver and the earthworm. Fifty thousand generations of freely roaming hunters left nature pretty much as they found it.

With the coming of herdsmen and tillers came man's

attack on the forests of the planet. Fire, having been stolen from the hearth of the gods, went its burning way to create new pastures and fields. But the maiming of the forest did not get into full swing until a hundred and fifty generations ago, when the iron axe was invented. The consequences were disastrous. Where forests were cut, fertile soil was robbed of its protection and the demons of erosion were unleashed.

Everywhere the drama has been the same. Man has mowed the forest, planted his grain, put his animals out to pasture. Fire and the axe have laid the soil bare; the tools of the tiller and the hooves of sheep and goats have torn it open. Wind has blown away some of the loosened earth, and along shaven slopes cloudbursts have washed much of it down into valleys and toward the sea. In many places rich topsoil, patiently hoarded over millions of years, has been squandered in a couple of centuries—and sometimes in just a few years. What has won praise at the moment as representing "progress" in human culture has often really meant, considered in the long run, an undermining of the foundation of this same culture.

The most delicate situations arose when forests were felled at the sources of rivers. The forest cover had kept the ground porous like a sponge, enabling it to serve as a water reservoir and as a constant source of renewal for rivers. When the forests were cut, the water balance was disturbed, and in many such places the vital udders of rivers went dry.

From the dark island outlines on a northern night in August one's thoughts may well drift toward another island world, dropping anchor for a moment at the island of islands, Ithaca, "the far visible one." Just as the old Norse poet described our archipelago as being grown-over with oak, so the Odyssey talks of Ithaca's lush pastures for goats and cows, "and here you also find all kinds of forest . . . and never-drying brooks." No more. Today the home island of the wily goat king-turned-seafarer is a rock-filled desert with bare hills and desiccated fields, furrowed by brooks gone dry. Ulysses yearned for home; the Ithacans of today would like nothing better than to emigrate from their used-up land.

Let Ithaca stand as a symbol of the whole classical archipelago. The poems of Homer and Pindar make it possible for us to sense some of the original beauty in their world: lush islands in a sun-bathed sea, a backdrop against which men erected temples, theaters, and homes. Sailing in the wake of Ulysses today, one meets a world that man has plundered and, for the most part, abandoned. Delos, the sun god's special island and once the richest, holiest, and most praised of them all, is now a treeless rock as naked, in Linneaus' truthful words, "as if it had risen a few years ago from the abyss of the sea." Islands described by Homer as wave-washed, fertile, beautiful—now sterile desert landscapes, with life and verdure remaining in some hidden valley.

In the same way, the Hellenic mainland tells with painful clarity how the migrant people from the steppes mishandled the beautiful land they found at the edge of the sea. It is a classical tragedy, severe in its lines, implacable. Where are the Arcadian forests in which the hinds of Artemis played and Hercules fought those wild boars? At one time more than half of Greece was covered with forest; today less than one twentieth is wooded. Hills once heavily adorned with trees have been peeled down to the bare rock. As early as five hundred years before Christ the destruction had reached such a point that Plato could write, shockingly, that "the rich and soft soil has run off and only the emaciated skeleton of the country remains." Today it is calculated that only two percent of the country's original topsoil is left. The hills of Attica are gnawed, dried-out, deflated; they are a strangely silent landscape in which the song of birds is not to be heard, for here there are no more territories for forest birds to conquer and to defend.

Deep down, the principal cause of the decline and fall of Greek culture must have been the devastation of the plant-bearing soil. One of man's great adventures began in a generous natural setting. The adventure's end is written in a ruined landscape.

And this particular drama, in which the Greeks, in a short-sighted effort to subdue nature, destroyed the very basis of their own existence, was nothing unique, nothing new, nor anything concluded once and for all. Greece was only an echo, resonant but dreary, of what had happened to the earliest human civilazations in the Mesopotamian twin river country. There, the Sumerian, Assyrian, and the Babylonian cultures foundered like wrecked ships in the sand or sank in the swamps. Over the Ur of Abraham and joyful Nineveh now lies an arid desert. The areas around the once mighty capital of Nebuchadnezzar have been transformed into marshlands—the result of intense irrigation by artfully built canal systems from the Euphrates and the Tigris, which packed the soil with salts through which the moisture could not penetrate. One of the little ironies of history is mirrored in these swamps. Alexander the Great, driven by the population pressures of his homeland into warlike adventures and the founding of a brief world hegemony, conquers mighty Babylon but is himself laid low by the new, the *real* masters of the region—a little malaria mosquito accomplishes what all the arrows of the Persians failed to do.

All the landscapes where human culture blossomed in antiquity tell much the same story today—a story of squandered growing-power and sapped juices. When the soil could yield no more, the foundations of flourishing cultures tottered. Everywhere the same expedients were tried when the limit had been reached. Of this, too, the Greeks provide classic examples. Overpopulation and mismanaged fields must have been among the incentives that led goat kings to become seafarers: it became necessary for them to seek from outside what their own land could no longer provide. Explosively, Alexander made efforts to widen his living space, but even earlier, in Homeric times, wave upon wave of people had been drifting westward in search of new land for their grain and their goats.

The classical theme has been repeated again and again ever since, without significant variations, in brutal monotony. Rome repeated the Greek drama on a Caesarean scale. The soil being drained in the campagna, the fields pressed on to the steep slopes of the Apennines, where the earth, laid bare, was washed into the valleys, muddying rivers and creating, among other things, the Pontine marshes, where once sixteen white cities had flourished. Soon Rome was forced to burst its borders; a power no longer able to sustain itself on bread and circuses had to admit that it was more needful to navigate than to live, and increasingly, bread-grains, olives, and wines were imported from beyond the water. Sicily having been thoroughly sapped, North Africa became the new great granary and a cornerstone of the world empire. And so Phoenician Carthage had to be destroyed to make room for the plows and triumphal arches of the Romans. In those days, the area that is now Tunisia harbored three times as many people as it does now—and so part of the empire it had to feed not only itself but also Rome. This proved to be impossiblew ithout a grandiose pillage of nature—one infinitely more thorough than the destruction Cato had preached. In due course, what the Romans had left undone was completed by the pasture herds of the Bedouins. Finally, where the soil had been ripped open, wind erosion opened the doors of the Sahara and the desert invaded the hundred-mile forests in which Hannibal had captured his war elephants.

Historians have preserved the memory of Alaric and his Goths; armed men pounding on the gates of a world empire have a greater dramatic appeal than shepherds and peasants leaving eroded soil behind them. But the real epitaph of the Roman Empire is written in the landscape itself: in those strange horizontal striations on the mountains of Sicily—remnants of once green terraces; in the withered crest of a Roman triumphal arch rising out of the North African sand dunes as an ironic monument to the very opposite of triumph; in pitiful clusters of clay and stone huts scattered over land on which mighty cities were once enthroned, all bearing grim witness that the impoverishment of the land becomes that of human beings too.

Last among the Mediterranean countries came Spain. The devastation there, when it reached the westernmost peninsula, was all the more thorough. The Spanish kings tried to build their empire on sails and wool. The forests were felled to gain lumber for new caravelles and new pastures for the enormous roaming herds of sheep, whose wool was to be transformed into riches for the royal treasury. The soil, which was to be the living foundation for power and glory, was wasted, and so today, as one flies over the ochre-hued peninsula, it is like watching a moon landscape of scalped mountains and dead riverbeds, a wasteland devoid of human response.

The history of the Mediterranean countries stands out in especially painful relief because the basic ideas of Western Civilization are so intimately associated with this region. But what happened there is, as if reflected in the shard of a mirror, what is still happening on a global scale. The fate of Ithaca, of the archipelago, of the world of classical culture, is about to become that of the whole world.

On the day when the lookout on Christopher Columbus' flagship sighted land, the same dreary old forces were set in motion anew. From the worn-out Old World a wave of people gushed westward, and surely it was no coincidence that the Mediterranean peoples were in the vanguard. At the meeting of races on the South American continent some of the original immigrants were themselves already trying to squeeze more out of nature than she was able to give; but the achievements of the Mayans and the Aztecs along such lines were innocent by comparison with the devastation that began with the first shipment of Spanish steel axes from across the Atlantic. What the new immigrants conquered came close to being an Eldorado—rolling forests protecting a rich soil, and crystal clear waters. Today, four centuries later, large portions of the promised lands of the Andes and the Antilles are wasteland; the forest cover has been peeled off, the topsoil has been washed into the valleys and carried away by rivers that are now a dirty yellow; enormous expanses of land have been eroded beyond redemption. The hunt for riches has ended in biological bankruptcy.

In a similar way, the European pioneers in North America assumed that here they had found a continent of unlimited resources. Prairies rich in buffalo and enormous forests were soon replaced by mile-wide wheat fields, cotton plantations, corn farms—and thus the soil was sucked dry almost as fast as it was taken from the Indians. The new immigrants shot, cut, and plowed their way farther and farther west, leaving depleted land behind them and not stopping until the Pacific Ocean called a halt to the westward movement—a movement that in truth had begun in ancient times, in the sea of Ulysses.

What took place in North America, in sum, was the usual violent exploitation of nature's riches. What had been gathered over many thousands of years was exhausted in the course of a few generations. In less than two centuries, fully a third of the North American topsoil disappeared down muddy rivers and off into whirling dust storms. The dramatic crescendo was that storm in the 1930's when for a whole week enormous dust clouds darkened the sky from the Atlantic to the Rockies as the wind swept away the exposed top layer of soil from five midwestern states, transforming them into desert and steppe. And erosion, unleashed by the farmer's zeal, still continues without mercy. Not too long ago, the United States Department of Agriculture reported that enough topsoil disappears each year to fill eighteen freight trains, each of them long enough to girdle the equator. Even today the sky over Canada sometimes turns black with clouds of dust blown all the way from Florida and Texas. Is it the foundation of a world power soon to be, quite literally, "gone with the wind"?

The largely virgin world that Europeans found in the Americas, the world they called "new," has aged very quickly. Europe to the north of the Mediterranean region, in contrast, was never forced to wear out its own soil so completely, since its population explosion occurred at a time when it was still possible to follow on a global scale the classical principle of the necessity of navigation. That is, northern Europe was able to export many of its people, while at the same time importing much of its food from other continents. As population pressure rose, the Americas were the first escape valves for northern Europeans, but tentacles were also extended to other continents. Asia and Africa both had to pay their tribute to the European pantry.

But Asia was an old world, already badly worn by its own people long before Europeans took much note of the area. The great cultures of Asia had begun to undermine themselves—also by abusing the soil—and Asia was a continent of overcrowding and hunger long before population problems became a current world topic. Failing to find the way out that Europe had found, i.e. emigration and colonization, Asia had to look for emergency solutions within its own confines. Thus, the continent which gave the world most of the domestic animals has had to kill most of its own, since it could not afford to let vegetable nutrients take the roundabout way through cattle before reaching man—the great exception being India's multitude of "holy" cows, gluttonously consuming the yield of the earth and never being eaten themselves. The majority of Asians have long been largely restricted to sustaining life on meager rice rations, to such an extent that in many ancient Oriental languages "rice" and "agriculture" are synonymous concepts. But now a critical stage is drawing near, as eroded wastelands grow apace with the population and the emergency solutions so far tried prove to be less and less adequate. Just in the course of the present century large areas of the Indian subcontinent have been laid fallow, the soil depleted of mineral nutrients. The earth of China, trampled by some ten billion people over thousands of years, has been subjected to horrendous wear and tear, despite the remarkable agricultural skills of the Chinese. Consequently, the Chinese are today streaming outside their famous wall toward Tibet, Manchuria, Mongolia, over the high plateaus against whose hungry hordes the wall was originally erected as protection.

Africa, the continent on which man first emerged, long remained a place of vast jungles and tropical rain forests. But even here the forests have been devastated to such an extent that only a tenth of today's Africa is shaded by a green roof of trees. Where forests were cut down, rivers have evaporated, the soil has dried out, and the temperature of the earth has risen by as much as sixty to seventy-five degrees —an increase sufficient to burn to death many of the bacteria that keep soil alive. And so each year hundreds of square miles of land are added to the Sahara and Kalahari deserts.

The disaster visited by man on Australia, the last continent to find a place on the map, was accomplished even more rapidly. Indeed, few areas display the chain of cause and effect in history as clearly as Australia does. In the middle of the last century, with the busy looms of Yorkshire demanding more and more wool, it happened that the supply from the traditional source, Spain, was much diminished in both quality and quantity—owing to the impoverishment of the Spanish soil. Australia obligingly came to the rescue of British weavers by opening its wide spaces to enormous herds of sheep. Soon the grass was eaten off down to the very roots, millions of sharp hooves pulverized the soil, and the wind carried it away. The consequence of the European hunger for wool was that in the course of just a century fully half of Australia's topsoil was blown into the Tasman Sea, and the island continent was left an Ithaca of colossal dimensions.

Thus, on a mental circumnavigation of the globe, undertaken on the beach of a leafy Swedish island, we find the classical drama repeated everywhere. In every part of the world, man has worn down the film of life, wasted this paper-thin cover which is the *sine qua non* of life in the borderland between the black deaths. Unwittingly, with little or no understanding of the meaning of our actions, we have been plunderers of our own nest. Over thousands of years, in spite of the visible evidence of ruined landscapes raising their mute but eloquent warnings along our path, we have continued to cherish the illusion of the indestructibility of the soil.

The good earth is life, life more primary and in its way more essential than that of individual vegetable and animal species, which are, after all, only secondary expressions of a living earth. Earth is a dynamic process in which mineral substances and water, worms and microbes, and air and used-up organisms are mixed, transformed, and renewed.

Its topsoil, produced so very slowly, can be consumed—diluted, impoverished, squandered in dust clouds over the oceans—all too quickly. Just as individual plant and animal species can be decimated or exterminated, so the life of the earth itself can wither and vanish—with ominous consequences for secondary life, the higher forms of life that have arisen out of the juices and salts of the soil.

This applies also to man himself. "My friend, who is not an offspring of the earth?"—a perspicacious question posed in the Babylonians' Gilgamesh epic. When we pillage the earth, we are simply indulging in an indirect form of cannibalism, one that is even more macabre than the direct version because it affects generations still unborn.

It is a strange, sham world that you see in all those widely publicized statistics that measure a country's prosperity in telephones and automobiles, television sets and cement production. One would do better to look at the Egyptian fellah carrying the mud of the Nile to his field in primitive buckets; or to catch a glimpse of the peasants in the Vosges who, each spring, in baskets on their backs carry back to their terraces the topsoil that was washed down by the autumn rains; or to read of farmers in the Balkans who send their children with table spoons to search the crevices for soil that can be rescued for their fields—one would do well to keep in mind pictures like these as reminders that our real capital is the earth. Consume that capital and bankruptcy threatens.

A central truth of our civilization is that its economy, like that of the earlier cultures that flourished and withered, is self-consuming. A central truth about ourselves as a species is that we have gotten out of balance with nature and become the only species in creation that is bent on destroying its own environment. Technology, an outflow of the human brain, has been used at an increasingly rapid pace to spoil, or even destroy, the very basis of our existence. In the present century, consumption of the planet's resources has reached truly sensational dimensions. In just a few recent decades more topsoil has been dissipated than during the whole of man's previous history. In the course of the last generation alone, fully one seventh of the surface of the planet has been transformed into desert and wasteland.

Not only have we worn out much of the world's soil. We have also disrupted the fundamental processes of nature herself. In order to give, the earth must receive. The circulation of nature is utterly implacable. What has come out of the earth must be restored, if the creative forces of renewal are to function. Procreation and decline have to be kept in balance. The Chinese have long known this simple truth, and for thousands of years Chinese peasants have been returning to the meager soil everything that has been consumed, so as to keep nature's circulation going. Everything was a loan to be repaid—the kitchen garbage, the excrement of man and beast, and finally the man himself, lowered into earth his hands had tilled and tried to keep alive.

It is precisely this organic circle that has been broken in many large parts of the globe. Deciduous forests, whose leaves were to have renewed the topsoil, have disappeared. The game animals have been decimated. Domestic animals are not allowed to return to the earth whence they came. Our own hygiene creates complications: flush a toilet and you rob the earth of a ration of mineral nutrients, while at the same time poisoning lakes and streams. From the point of view of the totality of nature, what the civilized individual thinks of as good sanitation is both a theft and a pollution. In this way, the earth is deprived of millions of tons of organic substances every day of the year—and vital water reservoirs are contaminated to boot.

What has happened, and is happening, is now beginning to be realized, at long last. Warning voices are being heard more often and more urgently, and there is a growing literature on the subject. Many countries have mounted efforts of various kinds to prevent the flight of the earth and to heal the grounds. Forests are being replanted at the well-springs of rivers, for example. But such efforts, up to now, have done no more than slow down man's ominous course; they have not changed its direction. On a world-wide basis, even now, more space is transformed into desert and steppe each year than is recovered or newly put to productive use. Moreover, civilization's assault on our topsoil continues on new fronts. Growing cities and suburbs, jet airfields, networks of highways— all deprive us of irreplaceable topsoil.

And while all that is going on, armies of chemists are mobilized in the hope that somehow they will find ways of artificially restoring to the soil the natural mineral nutrients that have been, and are being, drained and washed out of it. But scientists can imitate the processes of nature only in part. They can do little, for example, to foster the growth of microscopic life under the surface of the earth. So far, despite some strenuous efforts on their part, the total yields of man's fields over large areas of the world, even yields of poorer and less energy-laden kinds of food, are continuing to decline, as they have been doing for decades past. And so far only the feeblest beginnings have been made in the attempt to put an end to the wanton squandering of organic substances after they have paid a visit to our household— that is, to return the sewage to the earth or else transmute it into daily bread with the willing help of algae, microbes, or yeast fungi.

The most ominous point to be noted in this entire evolution is that man's destruction of the soil is, at bottom, an aspect of overpopulation. Thus, when a portion of the earth is worn out by man and his animals and can no longer yield sufficient food for them, the result is overpopulation. At the same time, an excessive population pressure leads to an accelerated attrition of the earth. Truly a vicious circle! Can anything be more important, can any task be more urgent, than making every possible effort to protect what is left of the earth's thin cover of topsoil, the prerequisite of life? But how are we to persuade the starving millions in overpopulated countries to refrain from squeezing the last ounce of food from their impoverished earth? When the navel touches the spine, who thinks of the deluge that may come tomorrow? Hence the paradox: the more people, the thinner the film which is to feed all living creatures.

Here another aspect, so far much neglected, opens up in the relationship between the have and have-not countries. Eating is not merely filling the stomach; it is also a matter of taking in balanced amounts of the elementary life-building substances. In this respect, too, the gap between rich and poor nations is widening.

The European peoples have recalled their colonial stewards, to be sure, but they still receive many vital nutrients from the increasingly eroded slopes and gradually starving fields of other continents. The man with the poor bowl of rice still gives Europeans some of their beef, milk, and clothing.

More than any other nutrient, we absorb protein. And protein, the primary building substance of life in the primordial sea, is about to be in very short supply in the world economy. World hunger is principally protein hunger. We, the upper class of the world, drink half the world's milk, eat three fourths of its meat, and capture almost all of its protein-filled oil-cake. On top of that, we take nine tenths of the wool in world trade—and wool is essentially protein. We Europeans consume, each of us, an average of forty-four grams of animal protein per day, while starving billions are having to do with only nine grams. Such is the imbalance of today's protein economy, in cold figures.

The exploitation of the earth and the population explosion can be summarized as a problem of protein, the primordial substance. The day will come, surely, when the hungry masses will lay claim to their share of the earth's protein supplies. On that day, perhaps, someone will simply proclaim that the protein taken out of the earth by flocks of sheep would be of better use if put in Asian stomachs rather than converted into clothing for the white man.

If the present world supply of animal protein were evenly distributed to all, each person would receive about twenty grams a day. By the turn of the century the production of protein will have to be doubled in order to maintain even this modest average standard, while if we do no more than maintain today's level of production everyone will be reduced to an Asian starvation level.

Nutrition experts are casting an eye on the earth's oil and coal deposits. After all, these substances contain stored waste products from life processes of ages ago and are, like all other remnants of life, filled with nutrients. A supply which could be transformed into proteins and vitamins is constantly being spewed into the air by our factories and motors cars. It just might be possible to get enough nutrition out of coal and crude oil to keep the problem of protein hunger at bay until about the turn of the century. This could give us a period of grace, but no more than that. The supplies of oil and coal are finite. Once we consume them we will again have used up capital that can never be renewed.

By the end of the century, world food production ought to be at least tripled in order to grant a tolerable nutrition standard to everyone—a standard lower than the one now enjoyed by upper class nations, but higher than that of today's starving billions. In many places it should be possible to increase the yield of the fields, but a higher yield would not necessarily mean an added supply of protein and other scarce nutrients. And there are no virgin lands to lay under the plow any more. It is no longer possible to move the

145

centers of culture to new regions and thus make a fresh start. Most of the productive portions of the planet are already in use. Less than a third of the earth's surface is considered arable, and most of that third—roughly twenty-eight percent of the total surface—is already field, meadow, or pasture. That leaves us no margin to speak of for breaking new ground to agricultural purposes—unless, of course, we decide to cut down the last of our forests. And that would indeed be a way to complete the tragedy in grand style!

Most of the forests that once covered Tellus have been burnt and cut down to make room for man's mismanaged fields, and forests have already become a rarity in many parts of the world. In Asia, for instance, there is only some thirty square feet of forest per person—and at century's end it will probably be down to a paltry ten square feet. Really productive forest now covers little more than an eighth of the surface of the earth, most of it along a northern belt from Canada over Scandinavia to Russia.

Considering the extent to which the forests of the planet have already been amputated, it is obvious that the remaining forests will soon be subjected to insuperable demands. In Scandinavia there used to be talk of the forest as the poor man's fur coat, but even Scandanavians are soon to learn "what a privilege it is to own one's own forest" to an extent that Linnaeus could hardly have imagined as he cast a melancholy eye over the naked islands of the archipelago.

With the world's population rising, the demands made on the world's forests will surely increase until every tree becomes a precious thing. By the end of the century, merely providing each inhabitant of the earth with a daily newspaper and just one book per year will require more paper pulp than the total of current world production—a somber perspective on the freedom of the press! And when the last silk worm has left its chrysalis, the last cotton bush harvested, and the last protein-rich bale of wool handled in the spinning mill, then the forests will have to play the principal role in clothing mankind. In our age of chemistry, they will be put to increasingly varied uses, and if we continue to direct our hunger for food against the forest, we will lose a large number of other commodities that we would rather not do without.

As descendants of the hunter, are we not also going to feel the need of the stillness that is to be found in our remaining forests? Can we afford to renounce what we have left of the riches of quiet?

Flickering questions in a quiet hour, as one sits listening to the play of the water around the boat.

Water has its own kind of stillness, different from that of the forest. It is a stillness that is almost always audible. Water is a multitude of sounds. The sea has its scale, the brooks theirs. I keep thinking of an early morning in the mountains, when we sat listening to the trickling and slurping of the water between grass tufts and stones in a tract where a river was born. Some of the officious litle drops that found their way in small runnels towards the Visa, to be forwarded from there to the Skagerrak, are perhaps in the waves now lapping at the *Thalatta*. For a little while they will play their part in the scale of the sea, even as they wait to be lifted by the sun into rain clouds that will drift back over the land and complete the hydrologic circulation.

And again the mind turns toward Ulysses' isle and its lifeless furrows, no longer rippling with what Homer called "never-drying brooks." A scale gone mute, a circulation broken.

In this sense, too, the fate of Ithaca is about to be shared by the entire globe.

For us in a land of a thousand lakes, the precious fluid

is still a matter of course. We simply accept this seeming abundance, rarely pausing to reflect on the decisive importance of water for the whole environment of man. The human body is two-thirds water—a reminder of our aquatic years. Water forms the larger part of our daily bread, whether it be the steak of·the rich or the rice of the poor. Large quantities of water have gone into the processes that lie behind the finished products on our table. Dr. Georg Borgström of Michigan State University, that Swedish Cassandra, has calculated that there are a hundred fifty quarts of water behind a single slice of bread, a thousand quarts behind each glass of milk. Water, though largely invisible, is present everywhere in my everyday existence. It is in the light I turn on at night, in the newspaper I open the next morning. The suit I wear in my daily work cost tons of water, the car I drive, hundreds of tons. No other single factor means so much to man as water does, both for his necessities and his luxuries.

In the million years that have passed since man rose above the savanna, he has been meeting water everywhere: in lakes, in rivers, in the veins of the earth. The supply seemed to be infinite and self-renewing. But today we know that the Homeric idea of never-drying brooks was an illusion. Just as some of the nutrients of the earth are beginning to be in short supply, so a global water shortage is now a threatening prospect. Hand in hand with his mindless depredation of the soil, man has perpetrated just as mindless a depredation of the earth's waters.

The first step was cutting down the forests, where the roots of trees and bushes had kept the earth porous and water-preserving while the crowns exhaled water into the atmosphere, enabling it to return in the form of rain. The forests having been cut, increasingly large areas under cultivation have cried for more and more irrigation. Finally, industry has demanded its ever-increasing tribute from the water reservoirs. In sum, the larger the harvests we try to squeeze out of the earth, and the more numerous the factories we build, the more water we use. Large portions of the globe have been living beyond their hydrologic means for a long time. Europe is currently using three times more fresh water than is supplied by hydrologic circulation, and parts of America are using many times more than that.

The predictable result is that many streams have run dry and many lakes been drained, evaporated, or overgrown. During the last generation alone, hundreds of lakes have simply disappeared from the map. Even such large ones as the Titicaca in South America and Lake Chad in Africa are rapidly shrinking in size. In just two decades the Caspian Sea, with an average depth in its northern part of hardly more than twenty feet, has dropped its level by almost seven feet. Many a large river has been choked or silted up.

But most precarious has been the pressure on the subsoil water. We know that there are subterranean rivers and lakes, but in our intoxication with space we have done precious little to investigate and map these wellsprings of life itself, and our knowledge of their rate of replenishment is poor indeed. Relying on the supposed inexhaustibility of subsoil water, we have emptied great reservoirs that had built up slowly over thousands of years, and we have drastically lowered the water table. In some places, zealous tillers of the soil have taken so much water out of the land as to lower the water table and drain the wells of other farmers miles away. Many a farmer has had to abandon his farm because of wells gone dry—indeed, some whole communities have lost their fresh water reserves. In some parts of the world water is a rare fluid that is rationed or sold by the glass. In California, where the water table has dropped fully a hundred feet in just fifteen years, the salt water of the Pacific may well be on the verge of invading the continent.

The situation is becoming desperate. The United Nations Educational, Scientific, and Cultural Organization has proclaimed a "hydrological decade" in an effort to rally the peoples of the world against the waste of water, but it is estimated that within a decade or so the population of the world will need two hundred and sixty-five trillion quarts more water than is currently being consumed—the over-consumption of today included. Thus, for large portions of humanity, water is about to become a question of life and death. World thirst following world hunger.

Earth, forest, water—the home, *our* home, which we are plundering. Three and a half billion people contributing to the wear and tear on the continents which our broom-finned ancestor from the Devonian sea conquered so long ago. And by the turn of the century, it is expected, the population of the world will be upwards of six billion . . .

To the southeast of where we sit, the lighthouses of Sneholm and Vattenholmen are flashing their cones of light over the fjord. Over our heads a few stars have been lit, fara-way beacons at which we can stare all night without receiving a bit of guidance—we can only wonder if living creatures in other worlds have found better ways of coping with their problems than we have. The sea is breathing heavily, as it has for ages, just as it breathed on the day it was known by the sun and made life light up.

We can look on the sea as a lost garden. Soon we shall have to return there, to another kind of amphibian existence, when the resources on land are no longer sufficient. After all, nine tenths of all photosynthesis in the green fac-tories of the plants is the work of little algae under the sur-face of the sea. In algae, seaweed, and plankton great re-serves of nutrition do remain, and in some hunger areas bread made from algae has already been tried. At present, only a hundredth of the world's food consists of fish—here, too, man's catch could be increased. And for man in the metal age, there are lumps of manganese and other minerals at the bottom of the sea; it is not likely that man will shun any means to get at such deposits, once he has touched the bottom of the barrel on land.

Thus we shall probably know in a not very distant future, sea gardens built along our beaches, harvesting the proteins of algae and seaweed—fenced-in, artificially manured pools in which mariculture will be carried on according to the agricultural methods we first learned to use on dry land. There has also been talk of fertilizing whole ocean tracts in order to increase the sea's productivity.

We will also have to find in the sea a drinkable substitute for the fresh water we have been pumping out of the continents. This will mean gigantic desalinization plants along the sea coasts, and enormous mains channeling the desalted water to our homes, fields, and factories. The first such stations have already been built.

The sea, generous and patient, will probably be able to restore to her prodigal sons some of what they have squandered during their sanguine existence on land. But not even the sea will be able to tolerate unlimited exploitation.

Our original home, the sea, is still an unexplored continent. We know less about it than we do about the surface of the moon. We are especially ill-informed with respect to the ecological laws of the sea—the finely balanced interplay between large organisms and small, the whole complicated pattern of the aquatic struggle for existence, the dependence of various forms of life on each other.

Reflecting on how man has abused and plundered the garden that once flourished across the continents, one may feel a certain fear that the balance of the oceans may be disrupted in a similar way when man returns to the sea on a broad front. Our enthusiasm is not undiluted, certainly, when we read of plans to turn certain blue deserts of tropical waters, now poor in fish and plankton, into rich new fishing grounds. Since this cannot be done by fertilizing the surface layers, the idea is to use atomic reactors in the deep to thrust the layers farther down, with their greater wealth of fish, toward the surface. Just who has made sure that this scheme is feasible without violating certain elementary laws of the sea? And the mind hardly dares touch on the political aspects of an unbridled nationalistic race for the sea's riches.

Even if the oceans still hold unpicked fruits in readiness, even if we are about to revert, in our economy, to some kind of amphibian life we will still remain tied to the continents on whose shores we were washed up so long ago. When the coelecanth went ashore, he gave us green thraldom as his legacy.

In the final analysis, we are fettered by our being part of the nature which we believe we are controlling. And there is an outer limit—through it may not yet have been quite reached—to what earth and sea can yield to a species seemingly bent on boundless, mindless multiplication of itself.

When earth resists, we try to act as our own Demiurge. Thus modern alchemists have promised that the waning supplies in nature's scullery will be replaced by artificial products. Even now there are more man-made variants of molecules than those nature has produced in her own experiments. The life-at-the-threshold-of-life that scientists have produced in their artificial primordial oceans gives some promise that the problem of producing proteins, carbohydrates, and vitamins may also be solved. Perhaps it may even be possible to imitate the chlorophyll magic of photosynthesis—to transform the salts of the earth into organic nourishment with the aid of sunlight and water.

But even the synthetic molecule has to be compounded out of the elements of the earth. The chemist may arrange the atoms differently than nature did, but he must build on the earth's yields of carbon, sulphur, and phosphorus. Further, synthetic production requires hundreds of times more water than is used in the laboratories of nature. No matter how far we advance with our artificial methods, nature's own factories will always operate much more flexibly than man's. Synthetic foods and desalted sea water can never be more than substitutes for what nature herself yields. Thus, as beings largely synthetically fed and clothed, billions of us milling about on a globe where ten thousand years ago a few scattered flocks of hunters roamed, we shall, under the very best of foreseeable circumstances, face a poorer existence than we would have had if only we had followed the laws of nature.

Beyond the island we can still hear the roar of the sea, this fluid filling the wide cups of the globe, as we enter the cabin. Night sneaks over the fjord, strong with saltiness.

It is good to fall asleep with the sound of waves lapping your eardrums. It reminds me vaguely of something almost forgotten . . . something far back in time . . . long before Ulysses . . .

8

. . . under the difficult
disc of the moon . . .

HALF ASLEEP, I HEAR THE NIGHT SWELL RUSTLING against the side of the boat. I sense it as something very distant, yet very near. It sneaks its way into ideas chasing each other through the hazy borderland between dream and wakefulness, cradling me in the half-slumber that clings unsteadily to fragments of impressions and thoughts from the day before.

I give a start, perhaps from a sleepy impulse I am trying to grasp, perhaps from some sound in the night. It must have been the latter, for now I seem to hear the wailing screech of the sea gull out on the fjord. It lasts for an eternity, and for the fraction of a second, and then nothing is heard but the rustling swell.

Opening an eye slightly, I see through the porthole that the moon, full or almost full, has risen over the small island called the Calf's Hide and spreads a staircase of quivering whitish gold over the fjord. At its edges the water merges with the night, blurring all rocks and land outlines and making them more to be guessed at than real.

The night is quiet but intense. It stands close by, yet keeps a distance so that I feel it as something timeless—something which is then, now, the future, and forever.

Again I think I hear, but now more clearly, the gull across the fjord. Peering toward the porthole again, I can see that the moon has risen higher over the Calf's Hide and pulled a bit to the right, in the direction of another rock in the sea. The outline of the white gold staircase over the fjord is changing all the time. Its flickering images quiver and change, dive down and return, disappear and make room for others.

I close my eyes again and allow myself to be cradled by the swell, retaining a picture of shimmering steps in the sea night, and it strikes me that if only we could climb that staircase, up toward the Lender of the Light, we might see our planet in better perspective.

We would soar far enough to see the earth satellite very large and shining overhead, just as it must have appeared soon after it had freed itself from Tellus and raised an enormous discover naked horizons and empty land masses—a spectacle never observed by man. Perhaps we would then see how the moon staircase ends somewhere beneath the Sea of Serenity, where the Lake of Dreams and the Lake of Death begin, reaching along barren ring mountains toward the Sea of Coolness at the pole of the luna globe.

As the observer turns around, he will be able to see, there in the black spatial indifference, our globe of nine movements, an accidental and very temporary home for me and for the sea gull, the hermit crab, and hunting bands of baboons.

If I now let the observer widen his pupils, he will perceive a bewildering multitude of milling, heaving, hungry life forms on the lonely spatial shred. Life taking shape in mushrooms and trees, in birds and fish, in beings crawling on the earth, or drilling their way through it, or walking on it. He will see life bubble up from sea and on land individuals who flash by for a moment and are replaced by others. A gamut of possibilities ranging from diminutive creatures, glimmering for a few experience-packed minutes or seconds, to patriarchal trees whose first green shoots began their rise back in the Bronze Age of man. In this multitude, life itself becomes the essential fact; its various forms are incidental.

The organisms comprising this heaving mass—tapeworms and dolphins, finches and human beings—are violently, pantingly, blindly preoccupied with propagating the seed of life, climbing on to each other, clinging to each other, emptying the fluids and seeds of life into each other or into the waters. The procedure of renewal has endless variations. There is a species of worm whose male, having found the female's sexual aperture, attaches himself into a lifelong wedding night. Insects among whom the female eats the male after receiving his gift, or other insects that die as soon as they have performed their propagating task. There are molluscs and conchs who free themselves of the sex organ and let it live an independent life with the female, and female seahorses who drop their eggs through long tubes into the sex pockets of the male, leaving *him* with the task of giving birth. Whales rise and lash the water with the violence of some force of nature as they give way to their passion in a meeting lasting a mere second or so. Armor-plated animals grope toward each other with horned shields clanging. Some birds stalk with ruffling feathers in a violent mating dance; others drop their wings smoothly into a protective tent over the solemn act. Male toads climb on to roe-filled females in nocturnal love trips into swampy breeding grounds. Hoofed animals heave over each other in panting lust; bipeds embrace in voluptuous pain. All are beings driven by the same common and mighty force, by the eros sounding the deep underlying chord in all that is alive—the urge to pass on the spark of life of individual and species. Even plants are forever letting pollen and spores whirl around; grains and fruits drop on to the soil—did not Linnaeus, the old master, believe that he could discern in plants "a kind of innate lust"?

The onlooker must also be reminded of something else that Linnaeus spoke of, on another occasion, as a law of nature "by which all abides under the disc of the moon looks out on mortal decay." For the other side of the great interplay of pulsating incitements in life is the relentless battle among individuals and species for the continued existence of their own particular variety. No species, vegetable or animal, can lead an independent life. They all live off one or more other ones, while the salts that maintain life incessantly pass from individual to individual, from one species to another. Each species has a relationship to another. The honey bee, the bird of paradise, the Bengal tiger—all derive the basis of their own lives from the lives of others. One species limits the next, and the merciless process of natural selection permits no species to grow beyond the basis of nourishment to which it has geared itself in the battle for existence. Just as death is the premise of life, so does the death of many individuals within a species constitute the premise of the survival of the species and the continuing diversity of living things.

Seen from the temporary vantage point of the lunar staircase, the cruel intensity of this drama is transformed into a harmony of orchestral might. The whole becomes a web of many finely spun checks and balances, whose threads weave together all that lives.

But then something moves down there and tears the web. A two-legged being, throwing off the cloak of checks and balances, disseminates himself everywhere, disrupting the harmony, gnawing at the globe itself, and soiling it. From our distant observation point in the staircase he looks like a skin cancer spreading rampantly over the face of the earth. The sea swell heaves. The sea swell rustles.

Something makes me open my eyes again. Now wide awake, I see it is my companion pottering about in the pantry; his lithe body is outlined through the cabin door. Now I remember; he was going out to see if he could hook a few whiting at dusk. He stayed out for quite a while and must have had a heavy catch to clean before turning in. The creaking of the dinghy as he returned was evidently what I just heard and thought was the cry of a sea gull.

The moon is over the Salt skerries now. I just had the idea that I saw it looming very large—as it must have appeared while it was closer and retarded the earth's violent rotation by using the tides as a brake. Since then it has receded, and it is continuing to do so. Someday it will spiral away from Earth, be captured by the attraction of the sun, and become the tenth planet of the system—but that will not happen for quite some time. Recently demoted by mapmakers into a sixth continent of the earth, hit by pea shooters from East and West, unwittingly embroiled in the prestige games of the super powers, waiting for the first human voyagers to erect their stations below its ring mountains—the moon will go on shining over billions of loving couples in various incarnations and fulfill the equally important task of generating heat on earth through the energy of ebb and flood, without which the earth temperature would be several degrees lower.

"Under the difficult disc of the moon . . . "—I am chewing on a refrain I once heard someplace. In reality, it is man himself who has made things difficult under the disc of the moon.

The skin cancer of the earth—this is something more than a sleepy thought under a clear moon one night among the islands. Through carelessness or unfamiliarity with the laws of nature, man has interfered with nature at an increasing pace for a bare ten thousand years, in ways that have broken checks and overturned balances built up over millions of years, and that have opened wounds and scratches on the face of the earth. To a species that has abolished the law of selection and proliferates at an accelerating pace, this interference has ultimately appeared to be even a "necessity"—a notion that is having ever-deepening consequences for the natural interplay in which man himself is a part.

Hippocrates, a man of clear vision in many respects, more than two thousand years ago spoke of earth, water, fire, and air as the four elements of the universe. Earth and water, sun and air are indeed the prerequisites of all life, and when we are careless in our use of any one of them, life becomes that much more difficult for our species and all the others as well.

We have monkeyed around with all these elements. The fire of the sun has been captured in man-made suns capable of extinguishing the life first ignited by the central body. The earth has been scarred, torn, and aged by mankind's efforts to procure food for ever denser masses of people; it has grown poorer and is growing still poorer every year. Our violent tapping of the globe's fresh water resources has gone hand in hand with an increasing pollution of the waters remaining. All over the world, but particularly in the industrial countries, hecatombs of sewage and industrial wastes are poured into lakes and rivers every day, with somber consequences for the organisms that are part of the aquatic nutritional chains. The biological balance of continental waters is being disturbed, and on populated coasts the effects are reaching far out into the ocean.

We have now reached the stage where in large parts of the globe there are no longer any clean surface waters at all. I recall a moment just a few days ago when I was lying prone across a rock filling myself with the pearly and precious fluid from a mountain brook. What a wonderful country where these things still remain possible! In countries deluged with people, such delights belong to the past.

The good earth and the pure water are about to become scarce commodities. Of air there is enough for the moment, but that too is being polluted. Wherever men have crowded together, in metropolitan cities and industrial areas, factory chimneys and automobiles fill the air with poisonous gases that millions of people have to inhale. Under certain conditions the effects of such gases may be lethal immediately; during one week of heavy smog over London, for example, four thousand more deaths occurred than would have been expected under normal conditions.

What a pathetic picture of the helplessness of modern man is that of the city dwellers in endless lines of cars moving toward beaches in search of reasonably clean water, while at the same time filling the air around themselves with poisonous exhausts.

The air around big cities and industrial areas has become an ever-growing dump. Increased population means increased urbanization. It also means an increase in the total consumption of energy. Rising "standards" means a rising consumption of energy per capita. More people and higher standards mean more waste of every kind—and with our present habits of consumption they also mean a progressive contamination of the air as well as of the waters.

There are also global effects, so far not easily interpreted, of the pollution of the air. The rape of the forests has reduced the natural production of oxygen. At the same time there has been a thinning out of the green cover which, by photosynthesis, could absorb at least some of the carbon dioxide blown aloft by our factories and motor engines. Every year a couple of billion tons of liquid and solid fuels are burned. The carbon dioxide thus set free has been accumulating gradually in the atmosphere. There it forms a hot-house ceiling that traps close to the earth a large amount of long-wave solar energy that would otherwise disappear into outer space, and at the same time makes it increasingly more difficult for life-giving ultraviolet light to enter our atmosphere from outside. Is it really possible to imagine that such progressive pollution of the air mass, our doing and no one else's, will not have consequences for us in the long run?

By our careless handling of the life-building elements we have destroyed a number of the balances built by nature. Man's view of nature has been dominated by considerations of what seemed to be immediately useful for his purposes. Urged on by a strong passion for simplifying nature, he has favored certain plants and animals and crushed or crowded out others. In this century alone, some sixty animal species have disappeared forever from the face of the earth, some of them eradicated directly, others the innocent victims of some transformation of their habitual environment that made them suddenly strangers in their own home.

Nature knows no closed spaces. In her economy, all organisms belong to one or another of a multitude of nutrition chains. Every time a species has disappeared or been forced back, a link has been broken in one of those chains. Sometimes it has been possible to see almost at once how nature has hit back. When the prairie dogs were forced out of the North American plains, for example, the fields were invaded by masses of grasshoppers and insects which the assiduous rodent had been eating and controlling. When the crocodile, that relic of the days of armor-plated giants and a creature considered holy by the ancient Egyptians, was decimated in the rivers of Africa, the number of protein-rich edible fish also declined drastically, because the water beetles, crabs, and predatory fish that live off edible fish but are, in their turn, a staple in the crocodile's diet now enjoyed a field day.

Above all, the agriculturist has always favored the crops

that seemed to be the most satisfying to his immediate needs, while regarding with indifference or open hostility other plants less directly useful. Our own century has witnessed a comprehensive transition to monocultures, to the one-sided cultivation of certain grain crops. The unforeseen effect has been to set the table for those insects, mites, and fungi that in the fight for survival specialized on these particular plants. In the enormous fields of wheat, corn, and alfalfa, they have multiplied to a degree that would have been utterly impossible in a more varied environment. It has been estimated that well over a fourth of the world's annual crop is being destroyed by such organisms and thus denied to the growing, and largely starving, world population.

Organisms appearing to be seriously detrimental to man must be exterminated, perhaps. But extermination means a kind of warfare, and during the past few decades we have been involved in a truly world war, albeit a stealthy and anonymous one. Until recently, however, we have been too preoccupied with the Cold War within our own species to notice that our chemical warfare against certain insects, fungi, and weeds was, in its effects, turning into a war against our whole environment.

A little something new in the old story of the careless habits of man on earth. The man of fifty carries pictures in his mind of the victims of poison gases in the trenches of World War I, but even so, he grew up in a world where the spread of poisons was not yet general. The seventeen-year-old pottering in the pantry has lived in no world other than one of widespread chemical warfare.

What started it was the discovery, during World War II, that DDT was effective in ridding soldiers of flies and lice. This disposed of at least one evil, and soon it was found that DDT could be useful for a number of other purposes. After the gunfire stopped, the DDT spray was made the weapon against a multitude of organisms considered to be pests.

162

With DDT it was possible to fight the mosquitos of the malarial swamps, with DDT forests could be dusted free of pinebark beetles, nun moths, and pine weevils, with DDT crops could be protected against a variety of insects. And soon we learned to produce a number of new and even more effective chemical weapons; in the United States alone some five hundred new preparations are introduced every year. Most of these products are synthetic, based on molecules hitherto nonexistent in nature. The experts speak of these things in terms of complex chemical formulas; for the layman it is enough to know the rather striking generic term *biocide,* meaning "killer of life."

This war by poison has reached extraordinary dimensions in a very short time. For every Kaffir hidden at the watering hole, his poisoned arrow in wait for the giraffe antelope, a hundred pilots are on the wing, spreading clouds of poison over the forests, and a thousand men with spray hoses are actively at work in the fields. The spraying mouthpiece, as a Swedish scientist has put it, is well on its way to becoming one of man's most important agricultural implements. The world is now subjected to a permanent showerbath of poisons, a counterpart of sorts to the radioactive fallout of the atomic bomb tests. There are life-killers everywhere around us nowadays.

At the outset, few people outside a tiny circle of experts sensed what was afoot. It was not until Rachel Carson sounded the alarm with her description of the frightening landscape of *The Silent Spring* that most of us suddenly awakened to our danger. Perhaps her warnings were a bit too sweeping, perhaps not, but if so, her alleged onesidedness was needed to direct our attention to what had been going on around us too long. In any case, many ecologists have since spoken out in very much the same manner. Even the vigilance of the daily press has been sharpened.

The warnings multiply. But the poison-war against nature continues.

What is really happening as these chemicals—thousands of tons of them every year—are poured over the planet's fields and forests and waters?

We know very little, so far—the war started so recently. In particular, little is known about the long-term effects of substances that did not exist in nature before and are thus outside the limits of biological experience.

But the effects that have already been observed are quite horrifying enough.

As a general rule, the efficiency of any biocide is judged simply by its ability to destroy a specific organism. The chemical industry is in a hurry—invested capital must yield revenue quickly and testing the effects of a new preparation on other organisms can be time consuming. Even as an immediate killer, a poison often strikes out blindly: the attack hits not only the intended enemy but also neutrals and allies—insects and plants that are harmless or even positively useful considered in human terms.

But the known and unknown indirect effects of a poison as it enters a nutrition chain can be far more disastrous. Our continuing insensitivity to the interrelation of all living things is truly astonishing. For example: bees and bumblebees, sucking nectar, suck poison from the flower cups in sprayed areas and die, leaving no way for pollen to be transported from flower to flower. Nature's own breeding process having been disrupted, the orchard trees in the area become sterile.

Or consider the worms that eat autumn leaves fallen from sprayed trees, an activity that will transform the leaves into topsoil. The worms absorb the poison in their bodies. Small birds eat poisoned worms along with poisoned insects and seeds, and die. Where fields or forests have been sprayed and dusted with biocides whole populations of small birds have been killed off in this way. The spring that Rachel Carson called "silent," a spring whose mornings have been robbed of the song of birds, is no mere figment of the imagination. In many places, nature has already lost some of her finest instruments.

From birds that eat seeds and insects, the poison is passed on to the predatory birds. Some of them die, and the eggs of still others remain unhatched in the nests, struck by the icy chill of rot where the warmth of life was to have pecked.

In America, robins and many other songbirds have become quite rare of late. Even the bald eagle, the national symbol, is about to vanish—made incapable of reproducing, it is believed, by life-killing chemicals that have accumulated in testicles, egg tubes, and unhatched eggs.

Many poisons have proved unexpectedly long-lived, and during their migration through a chain of nutrition such poisons may be progressively accumulated until they finally reach amazingly high concentrations. Thus, it matters little that a poison may be spread over the land in highly diluted solutions, or that it is "guaranteed" by the manufacturer to be harmless to higher organisms "if used as directed." As the poison wanders from link to link in the nutrition chain it can become concentrated into lethal doses. It can be passed on from generation to generation, from species to species, hoarded in tissues and vital organs, long after it has ceased to have any affect on the environment where it was originally spread.

It has been possible to observe such migration and accumulation very clearly in the aquatic nutrition chains. When a life-killing liquid or solid is spread over fields and forests, some of it always accompanies drainage water into rivers and lakes. There, invisible plankton enrich the poison in their simple organs; water fleas and other small organisms feed on plankton; and in due course the poison is passed along to small fish and then to predatory fish in ever-increasing concentrations. Suddenly an inexplicable mass death of fish occurs—a "fish kill," the newspapers call it. Or perhaps some of the poisoned fish are eaten as prey by feathered or furry animals. Thus, a biocide intended for a small insect in a forest or field may well be the death of the salmon, the grebe, or the polecat.

The country hardest hit by the assaults of these poisons is probably the United States, but there is now biological insecurity everywhere, in one degree or another.

On the Swedish landscape for example, it is no longer a rare experience to come upon dead birds, their bodies tensely bent backward after a death agony, or dying birds reeling about because their legs and wings are unable to function properly. Investigating a number of such cases, the School of Veterinary Medicine in Stockholm invariably found large concentrations of mercury in both seed-eating birds and the predatory animals that feed on them. The evidence clearly pointed to a mercury-treated seed grain used in Swedish farming to protect crops against mold fungi. The government intervened, but already, in the short span of a few years, maps showing the distribution of Swedish birds had been rendered grossly misleading. The yellow bunting, the sea eagle, the stannel hawk, the horned owl, and the hawk are all about to vanish from the Swedish landscape, all of them victims of death by mercury—our spring is also getting more silent. And through the release of industrial wastes, alkyl compounds capable of affecting the brain and the central nervous system are entering Scandanavian waters; alarming concentrations have been found in both fresh-water and Baltic fish.

The plain fact is that we have entered a period of accelerated contamination of our entire environment. The industrial countries form the vanguard and, not unreasonably, the extent of a country's environmental contamination has been adduced as a yardstick of its civilization. In this whole process, the increasing pollution of water may be the most alarming development of all. Nowhere on our planet does water exist naturally in isolated containers. Surface and subsoil waters are constantly on the move, interconnected by innumerable hidden waterways, and in a very real sense the world's water resources constitute one continuous whole. Thus, water pollution simply cannot be localized. If biocides are spread on surface waters, no matter whether by carelessness in connection with the spraying of woods or farm lands, or deliberately in order to exterminate so-called trash fish and inconvenient bottom vegetation; or if the life-killers seep into the subsoil water through the fine capillaries of the earth and thereafter spread in secret—it is all the same. Suddenly, mysterious deaths by poison may occur in a spring lake, or wells are found to be poisoned far from the spot where the life-killers were originally disseminated. Nobody really knows from where the poison came, but it is there.

The contamination process is aggravated by a phenomenon that has only recently been recognized. Most preparations involved in this chemical warfare were put on the market without having been tested in nature. It now seems that when they are unleashed nature's own laboratory often takes charge. Having been provided with substances to work with that she did not have before, nature sets about rearranging atoms and building new molecules. It has been found that nature, even when working with a couple of relatively harmless biocides, can build new compounds that are many times as poisonous in their effect—perhaps fifty times as poisonous.

Oftentimes, as we now know, the life-killers per se are not needed to produce such effects. Sewage and industrial wastes poured into lakes and rivers can be transmuted, when exposed to the influence of water, sunshine, and air, into some new harmful substances. And if artificial life-killers are added to such a witches' brew already fermenting in the great retort of nature, the concoction hardly becomes more wholesome.

In sum, the use of biocides in the fight to save crops for hungry human stomachs can be extraordinarily risky and costly, so much so that in the end the immediate gains achieved—protecting this or that crop from pests—are proved to be illusory. Our technically efficient weapons have all too often become boomerangs that turn with renewed vigor back against ourselves. By exterminating certain species, we replace nature's multiplicity by a simplified system that is likely to be highly vulnerable. Where one insect pest has been eradicated, other pests, previously existing only in small colonies, can increase in numbers and devour whatever is offered at the banquet table. Once-harmless insects can suddenly become scourges.

Perhaps even more significantly, man's interference in the processes of natural selection has had the effect of creating new strains of the very insects he thought he had rendered harmless—new strains that are resistant to the biocides. Insects, after all, have had some three hundred million years of experience in adapting to changing conditions. Most species show a broad range of variation; some are weak, but others are tough and can become even tougher through mutation. Poisonous assaults by man may weed out the weak, but some of the toughest survive to form new strains, immune to the poisons that had exterminated the rest of their species. Because of their brief life span and their great powers of proliferation, such insects can quickly multiply and mount their assault on the crops in new and effective armadas. Thus, for example, the malaria mosquito, once apparently under control in large areas, has developed new strains that are resistant to DDT and are perhaps about to undo the post-

World War II victories of the World Health Organization.

Fields and forests are now being stormed by new strains of old insects that are invulnerable to DDT and all other existing biocides. These new attacks are being felt all the more strongly because some of nature's own defensive walls have already been razed. The birds that would have kept the insects in check have largely disappeared. A titmouse family, multiplying normally, eats about a hundred sixty-five pounds of insects in a year, a swallow family with five young can eat some half-million individual insects in a few summer months. Where the song of birds has been silenced, we must expect invasions of insects surpassing anything yet experienced by mankind.

And what are we to do? Create new, even more poisonous substances to pour on nature, with new, scarcely imaginable consequences?

The most alarming feature of this problem, as of so many others, is that we know so little about the likely consequences of what we are doing. Man is meddling with the processes of nature everywhere today, often with little or no understanding of the forces with which he is dealing.

Sometimes all goes well. Before the first hydrogen bomb was detonated over a Pacific atoll, there were reputable physicists who feared that such an explosion might start a chain reaction in the oceans. It did not happen, but it was not until long after the experiment that the scientists' uncertainty about its effects was made known to the public. A couple of years later, when a bomb was to be exploded inside the newly discovered Van Allen belts, prominent astronomers warned that such a surgical incision might change the order of nature for a long time. The bombed-out hole in the magnetic girdle was filled within hours, as it happened, but the stakes had been high in the gamble.

There are many other examples of our ignoring the

possible effects of our meddlesome experimentation. In the days of the bomb-test psychosis, a number of heavy nuclear loads were exploded in outer space, the largest one equivalent to fully a fourth of the total energy of the Van Allen belts. We still know so little about the laws of space that no one is able to say with certainty that such bangs will not shake, or have not shaken, the delicate balance built up over millions of years in the outer atmosphere, causing disruption in climate.

It is not difficult to see in retrospect how our itchy fingers on nature's wealth have produced alarming effects. Ignorance of the laws of nature has led to the destruction of fertile land, to the emptying of subsoil water tables, and to a pollution of the water resources of the globe so extensive that it is becoming one of the vital problems of the human race. Likewise, the continuing chemical warfare against insect pests has already had a number of consequences that were not foreseen. The long-term effects are still shrouded in obscurity, and we know little or nothing of what may be happening, unseen, in the film of life itself—because the very earth we walk on is now impregnated with our poisons. In some responsible quarters, the diminishing agricultural yields of the land have been ascribed to disruptions in the delicate balance of micro-organisms in the topsoil. Not much of such disruption has been mapped. But ignorant as we are of how our spreading of poisons may affect the life of microbes in the topsoil left to us as the prerequisite of our higher life, we continue to gamble.

At the end of the nutrition chain stands man himself, and no great powers of imagination are needed to realize that ultimately the poisons must reach him too. He is, after all, omnivorous; he feeds off the crops of the earth and the bodies of fish, birds, and mammals. Now, for the first time in history, he risks encountering poisons everywhere in his daily life. They may turn up, invisible, on his dining table: in milk, butter, and cheese from cows pastured in fields sprayed with DDT; in the meat of game; in eggs laid by hens that have pecked at mercury-treated seeds; in the beef of cattle filled with antibiotics against epidemic diseases and with tranquilizers to keep them calm so they will not lose energy and weight; in a fillet of fish; in a leaf of lettuce, in water. Each dose is perhaps insignificant of itself, and it is at least conceivable that the danger of life-killers in our most common foods has been a bit exaggerated by some. But poison *is* poison, even in small quantities, and more and more scientists are abandoning old theories about thresholds of safety and harmless doses. These poisons can accumulate in the human body, and even the smallest dose represents an addition to the accumulating charge.

Almost all the foods we buy are in some way processed, usually by the addition of foreign substances. We hardly ever experience the taste of a pure product of nature. Each day we absorb with our food several grams of chemical additivies. Their widespread use has come about too recently for anyone to know what the long-term effects will be. But for a human being to absorb into his system, in the course of an average lifetime, chemical additives in an amount almost equal to his body weight—surely this must put a strain on the organism that was not visited on earlier generations. We cannot exclude the possibility that some of these substances may in the long run cause degeneration of vital organs.

Some of the life-killers—DDT is a notorious example—are stored and accumulated in man's body fat. Today, most members of the human race probably carry DDT in varying amounts, and it has been said that only the members of an Eskimo tribe living on the outer rim of Alaska may be entirely free of it. Doctors fear that certain preparations—found not only in food but also in moth-proofed fabrics, in plastics, and in insulating material—may affect the formation of cells and cause cancer. Nothing has been proved. But whatever the facts may turn out to be, we have no letters-patent certifying that there is no connection between our chemical-imbued environment and the increasing incidence of cancer, particularly among the young.

In regard to possible genetic effects of the progressive storing of poisons in the body, we are still groping in the dark. We know that seeds from sprayed plants have been capable of producing abnormal plants. We know that in some animals life-killers may enter the sex cells, break down chromosomes, and change inherited properties or cause sterility, so that insects have mutated and birds have lost their capacity to multiply. We have no certain proof, so far, that the genetic heritage has been changed or destroyed in animals of a higher order. But one may wonder why genetic effects should be restricted to insects and birds. The thalidomide cases proved that there are preparations that can cause malformations in new-born human beings. Nobody can exclude the possibility that some of the preparations now being spread in our environment will have effects comparable to radioactive fallout.

If that proves to be the case, we are threatening our own property and our heritage from still another front.

Some years ago, when certain powers filled the atmosphere with radioactive particles that were carried around the globe by winds, they committed, in effect, a kind of peace-time aggression against the whole of humanity. We might say, with the same justification, that we are involved in chemical warfare against ourselves. When one well-known scientist can speak of the present distribution of poisons as "the greatest threat to life on earth," and another scientist can call it "a danger to the human race greater than that of a third world war and the atom bomb,"the layman has reason to feel alarmed.

172

As he observes his own environment in the process of incessant deterioration, the layman is surely entitled to raise a few pointed questions. After all, the elements that build and protect life are eminently the property of all living beings. Air, water, and sunshine belong to everyone. No one can really *own* soil; he can only temporarily administer part of what is essentially capital resource held in common.

Does not every passenger in existence, who must count this globe as his home for a short while, have the right to *demand* that no part of the common capital be squandered, that his natural environment be not impoverished, that the life-bearing element be not impaired?

By what right do others allow themselves to foul the air I am breathing, the water my tissues need, and the food whose salts are to nourish me—to foul these things with radioactive particles or other substances hostile to life?

If we have reached a stage where we cannot do without life-killing elements in our struggle to utilize the resources of the globe, do I not have the right to demand a clear statement of profit and loss for the totality of which I am a part—an accounting, based on solid facts, of the consequences for the balance of nature to which I belong, and for the nutrition chains in which I am a link?

Must I, *can* I, condone passively someone's gambling with my environment in a way that may jeopardize the very core of our species—whether the gambler be a superpower or an anonymous fellow wanderer?

A man with his future behind him does not raise such questions in his own interest. But just now I caught a glimpse of a young man through the cabin door. For a short while it has fallen upon me to manage a small portion of the joint heritage of the human race—the genes that began forming even in the primordial sea. I have been allowed to be a small link in the bridge connecting everything bygone with the future. It is not unimportant to me that this bridge remain standing.

My companion has tiptoed inside and turned in. I can hear his even breathing from the bunk to port. It mingles with the sounds of the night outside, with the rustle of the swell.

The moon is still out there, indifferent to man's difficulties. Night has closed around an earth vulnerable to our actions, our urges, and our misconceptions about our own place in creation.

What has gone wrong, probably, is that we have failed to see ourselves as part of a large and indivisible whole. For too long we have based our lives on a primitive feeling that man's "God-given" role was to have "dominion over the fish of the sea and over the fowl of the air and over every living thing that moveth upon the earth." We have failed to understand that the earth does not belong to us, but we to the earth.

It was a mistake for us to believe that we could control nature. We can only change it—and, almost without exceptions, the changes we have wrought have been for the worse. On nearly every page in the book of nature we have imprinted a *cave hominem*—Beware of Man! Our interference with nature has led to a disrupted natural balance, to devastated lands, to poisoned waters, to air with less oxygen content, to incessant deterioration of our environment all the way to a global cancer, which now forces us to begin to discover that our own existence as a species is finally threatened.

We have been working against nature, not with it. Ours has been a frivolous activity, and it may have dire consequences.

9

*". . . nothing less
than mankind . . ."*

HOLMEN GRA—"THE GRAY ISLE." LAST STOP ON OUR
late-summer trek. To the north, a glimpse of Klädesholmen,
bright in the dusk. A few miles behind us, in the Hakefjord
inlet, the white fishing village of Astol clinging to a treeless
rock. Human homes turned toward the sea. Outrunners of a
society to which we shall return tomorrow. To the southwest,
the Pater Noster skerries extend their rosary of sea-washed
rocks and shoals, against which the swell breaks lazily. In
front of us the sea, open all the way to the horizon. The sun
is a few degrees above the rim to the west.

We are sitting on a rock ledge between a pair of cairns,
built high on a crest as is customary in the mountains. The
archipelago is essentially an extension of the mountain landscape—another mountain world in which only the peaks
reach out of the water. The lines are different, of course; the
dominant features of the actual mountains are vertical and
diagonal, whereas everything in the island world rests on the
line of the horizon. And there is a different tone to the wind

as it plays on the water. There is a fresher bite to the breeze, and the gale winds play on a more somber instrument here than when forcing their way through a mountain valley. But the expanse, the view, the refreshing feel of wide, open space is the same on the shore and in the mountains.

The Gray Isle—barren, with only a little sedge grass, thistle, wild pansies, and stonecrop finding a clawhold in the crevices—has become our Fanaråken among the island mountains.

Seagulls circle in excited flight overhead; their screeching reverberates in the silence of the sea. We recognize the sentry call of their living space. The territory of the gulls is among the tufts of sedge and the white-stained rock ledges below us, and one must be wary when entering this domain, particularly in the hatching season. Like men, the gulls drop bombs against intruders, and their marksmanship is good.

Except for the excitement in the gull colony, we would have complete stillness around us.

The outer belt of the archipelago can still afford us some of the same kind of seclusion that we find in the mountains, only a bit more fragile. As we sailed our *Thalatta* over the blue expanse, landing briefly on uninhabited islands and roaming over their rocky surface, we felt the privilege—just as we had during our mountain hike—of living at a time when it is still possible to find quiet and privacy. Just as in the mountains, we were seized at times by an almost indescribable feeling of having somehow come closer to our origins.

My companion has been given the opportunity to meet the sea as often as possible throughout his seventeen years. He fits easily and naturally into its rhythm, and his observations are intense. During a day in the sea breeze, his retina photographs his impressions, and afterwards he is able to unreel them as though they were on film, omitting not a rock, buoy, or change in the wind.

Sitting here together, taking our leave of the sea, we recall some of the sights and impressions of the last few days.

—Early mornings, when we tumbled out of the cabin and dived straight into the water, and then set out into a lifting haze in which the skerries and buoys within range of our eyes seemed to hover weightlessly above the surface of the sea.

—The St. Elmo's fire sparkling one night at Soteskar in a way that made the whole fjord seem phosphorescent.

—Robinson Crusoe days on the Weather Islands—the pair of us sunburned, salt-drenched, taking our meals directly from the pantry of the sea: mackerel smoked over juniper twigs between a couple of rocks on the beach, or codfish thrown into the kettle straight from the sea so that none of the salty freshness is lost.

—The birds that followed us. Eider ducks lifting heavily from the rim of the water. The fearless sociability of the snipes, drilling their awl-shaped beaks into the bottom silt along the beaches. A skua in pecking pursuit of a gull on the wing until the gull throws up the contents of its craw, which is acrobatically caught in midair by the skua, while the rest of the gulls observe a strict neutrality until it is their turn to pay tribute to the little pirate. Just once, a peregrine falcon sailing proudly as if there were no death by mercury. Another time, a flock of herons on their flight south.

—Days when the sky was brittle as crystal, with an inlay of a few feathery cloud specks in its blueness. Other days when gray cloud bags suddenly burst open and poured a content of unexpected abundance over us—and the freshness afterwards.

And now, in the waning evening breeze, the Gray Isle. A few moments in the land of wandering dusk, before night moves its cloak toward the horizon.

The stillness of the islands is never felt so intensely as in the serene hour that prepares most living creatures for darkness and rest. But there is also something hectic in the colors that mark the sun's farewell for the day, much as there is in the flaming landscape of autumn just before its death. The skerries, gray in daylight, burn in bronze or—at the water-line washed clean by the sea above the living space of the sea tulip—in shades of light ochre. For a brief moment the sea is like molten copper in the path of the sun—and all at once the colors are extinguished.

What an extraordinary mixture of awesome stillness and feverish glow is offered by the sea in the evening, just before daylight dies! In the land of the evening is my quiet. Also my disquiet.

> The sun turns black,
> earth sinks in the sea . . .

Such is the atmosphere of sunset evoked by Voluspá of the ancient Icelandic Edda. In the somber visions of the seeress, the *vala,* the setting sun is used to illustrate something definitive, the end of our saga. The rest of the vision could be a description of the nightmare of our own times—that of man-made suns threatening mankind with cosmic destruction.

> Fierce grows the steam
> and the life-feeding flame,
> till fire leaps high
> above heaven itself.

Visions of a sunset of mankind have deep cultural roots. They are found in the most ancient of our myths, side by side with our dreams of a vanished golden age. Such visions were present in the Hellenic legend of the falling golden ages being brought to a violent end by Cronus. In the Hebrew vision of Armageddon, in which the sun burns men like fire, all islands disappear, and the mountains cease to exist. In the Ragnarok story of Voluspá.

Earlier ideas of destruction were often based on the feeling that the end was close at hand. A collective panic sometimes occurred when an omen was interpreted as a presage of the imminent end of the world. But each time the globe rolled on and mankind remained on it. No closing notice was posted.

Today, however, man's fear of doomsday has substance as never before. It is not a matter of shapeless horsemen of the Apocalypse galloping under the clouds. What is ominous is not just a sign in the sky that the ignorant find hard to read. Man's present fears are based on ironclad facts. The intertwined problems of unleashed destructive powers, the population explosion, and the accelerated rape of the soil and of the air we breathe appear to thrust us with ever increasing speed toward a critical climax.

The thin film of life is being worn out faster with each decade as the human masses living off the resources of the globe continue to grow. At any moment the two curves may cross each other and go their separate ways—if indeed they have not done so already. If in such a situation the old pattern of the battle for the territories is to be followed—if there is to be a fight by all against all for the planet's limited crops, water, and space—then it is hard to convince oneself that the result will not be global chaos, a convulsion in which the very forces that put the first club in the hand of Makapan man will release weapons of extermination even more destructive and bestial, perhaps, than those we have already come to know. We have reached a stage where we have come so dangerous to ourselves as to create for the end of our saga a Ragnarok beyond all powers of comprehension.

Was perdition foreordained in the big brain given in the Ice Age to the erect animal, the species that would presume itself capable of controlling nature?

Other species have perished because they were overspecialized. The enormous armor-plated body of the dinosaur was one such evolutionary mistake. Will the big brain of man prove to be something too heavy for him to carry—not a triumph of evolution, but one of its fiascos?

In its fourteen billion cells, our brain has stored ever more perilous knowledge while increasing our technical capabilities. But knowledge is not wisdom. An Oriental myth of creation had man being chased from the Garden of Eden as punishment for his tasting the fruits of the tree of knowledge. Cicero believed knowledge to be what the sirens used to tempt Ulysses so powerfully that he had to have himself tied to the mast of his ship. It is as if the ancients who gave us our myths knew intuitively that knowledge unbridled by wisdom can be dangerous in the extreme.

Cosmically speaking, it would be no great tragedy if man were gathered with other species in the boneyard of frustrated hopes—provided that he did not take with him a large portion of the rest of creation. Man is less necessary to the whole of nature than the earthworm. Nor can we know what other unknown possibilities may yet be hidden in ocean and jungle—possibilities that might be able to come out into the open if man departed from the scene.

But as a link in mankind, as a bearer of some of the collective heritage of genes which it has been my task to pass on, I am unable to accept stoically the idea that the catastrophe is unavoidable. Within certain limits, man possesses a free will. From free will follows choice—the power to choose between alternatives. To accept the triple threat facing us today as something inevitable is to make a passive choice that may ensure disaster—whether by way of a sunset of the entire species or, in a new barbarism, in a merciless battle, flock against flock, perhaps even among beings who have been transmuted, through man's own actions, into a race quite different from our own.

What threatens us is no twilight of the gods. There will be no Ragnarok unless man stages it himself. But if, in a world where the possibility of destruction has become a reality, we persist in letting our actions be governed by obsolete ideas and patterns of behavior, we run the risk of making the ultimate disaster merely a matter of time. It can be averted only by a radical adjustment of our ideas and actions to the fundamentally different conditions which we ourselves have created.

The adaptation needed for survival is one of enormous dimensions. For it is our torment, and our adventure, to live in an age of change that is more rapid and probably far more radical than the transformations of ten thousand years ago, when the hunter emerged from the forest and became a settler. At the same time, our predicament is not comparable to any other in mankind's short history. For we are now pressed to make choices that concern mankind's very survival. Our future, our whole existence, may well be decided within one or a very few generations.

Should not our awareness of this stimulate our urge of self-preservation to efforts beyond any hitherto attempted by our species?

When man was washed ashore on the beach of consciousness, he was faced by the enormous task of finding his own way. Formed on the same anvil as everything else in creation, he became unique in the sense of being able to break down some of nature's fences so as to influence his environment and thus the conditions of his existence, rather decisively. Heretofore this capacity has been exercised more or less blindly. The task remaining is to learn to steer it according to a plan, with open eyes.

It is possible that man, as a biological phenomenon, has reached his ultimate phase of development—provided he does not destroy, by carelessness or in despair, the genetic heritage that has been gathered within him over the eons. It may be that his social organization is what requires new evolutionary changes and that through such changes, consciously effected, we still have a chance to modify our own destiny.

Bands of hunters, the first city states, the superpowers of today—man's attempts at social organization have been hardly more than one imperfect experiment after another. No society has ever attained the stability of a beehive or an anthill. Everything has been fluid, an experimentation with various doctrines and social contracts. And so it remains.

A constant factor among the many attempts at organization has been the rivalry of different communities: flock against flock, state against state, alliance against alliance— the territorial pattern that has been with us since the most primitive, inarticulate stages of our existence. It is this constant that must be overcome, somehow, if man is to succeed in creating a viable social organization.

Behind us a pair of islands glow under the slanting rays of the sun. Curiously, they are named Berlin and The Wall— names that call to mind "walls" that have been erected and "curtains" that have been lowered between various factions of humanity. As fossils from earlier ages or as current reflections of fossil thought patterns, dividing lines make of our planet a checkerboard on which boundaries drawn by strength and accident mark off what is unconditionally "mine" and conditionally "yours."

In an era of migration of peoples, the boundaries drawn by a tribe that took possession of an area may have corresponded originally to distances and temporary conditions. Until quite recently it was sometimes enough for a local *condottiere* to establish personal rule over whatever territory he happened to be able to capture—and so came into being a "state" with a name of its own, national symbols, and eventually a national spirit. Most national states, these relatively new products of man's social experimentation, came into being at a time when the horse and the sailing ship, or at best

182

the steam locomotive, were the principal means of transportation. The same pattern has been followed in our own day and age, and our hurried creation of new states has often been done in terms of boundaries that were originally drawn, more or less arbitrarily, by colonial powers decades or even centuries ago.

Today, with the increasingly populous continents drawn so much closer to each other, the world has become too narrow for the old frontiers. It took Magellan's *Victoria* three years to circle the globe; Jules Verne had his resourceful Phileas Fogg do the trick in eighty days; and now it is possible to follow the sun around the world in supersonic airplanes. It took our grandparents forty-five minutes to travel six miles by horse-drawn cart; today's astronaut covers half the earth in the same length of time. Thus, the old measurements of distance have become imaginary lines on the map, and the clock has replaced the mileage gauge in measuring distances. The real distance that separates us from the most remote spote on this planet is best understood in terms of forty-five minute points on a watch dial.

These points remind us how small the world is, in which the multiplying millions have to exist. They recall the totality into which we have been hurled—the fact that the evolution towards differentiation, which began with scattered bands of hunters gradually taking possession of the earth, has been superseded by a violent trend toward global uniformity.

Just a few generations ago the world was enormous and man's problems were limited. Today the globe has shrunk and man's problems are boundless. To solve the problems we now face, our "community" must be nothing less than mankind as a whole. Viable relations must be created, not just between nations and individuals as before, but between mankind and individual man.

Ages ago man met the challenge posed by ice-age climatic changes by abandoning his nomadic forest existence

183

and settling down in communities, which were to develop from primitive beginnings into the modern national states. Man must now meet the new challenge—one that is of his own making—by forming a new social organization that is global in structure and function. For without some kind of world governance we cannot hope to master our problems, irrevocably interwoven and global as they are, and our destiny.

To a generation that sucked in the idea of the sovereign state with its mother's milk, the notion of world government may seem utopian—almost as unreal as the Homeric account of the lingering golden age island of Scheria, land of the Phaeacians and symbol of the Hellenic dream that the earth would one day be transformed into a luscious garden of peace and wisdom. But it is nothing new that the Utopia of one generation may be recognized as practical necessity by the next. Everything ultimately depends on our ability to deliver ourselves of emotions and ideas that once had a function in our battle for survival but have since become useless.

The universal fear of nuclear war and the pressing demands of starving millions for equality may both prove to be psychological forces preparing us for world government. In both, there is an appeal to reason.

Listening this evening to the gentle swell from an ocean strangely close and seemingly large, one can almost hear again, echoing in the mind, the measured step of countless young men in uniform resounding around the globe. Is this echo through the stillness the final Grand March of an era? When an aggressor must expect to be devoured by the same flames he sends against his victim, when national security has become an illusion because our weapons are capable of sterilizing the entire globe—at that point war has taken on a dimension of irrational lunacy that ought to make it abolish itself. Equally insane in a world of shortages is the wholesale waste of vital raw materials, productive resources, and human

184

intelligence on armaments—a waste calculated in abstract monetary symbols at two hundred billion dollars every year.

It is hard to see how this spiral of collective lunacy can be reversed without depriving the nation-states of that sovereignty which they symbolize so fittingly with images of lions, eagles, and other beasts of prey. Disarmament, trimming the talons of the beasts, must of course be global in scope, for if any major nation refuses its cooperation, the game is up. Thus it must be carried out by stages according to a balanced plan; perhaps it can be only symbolical at the start, so as to reduce distrust, and then more practical. It must apply to all arms, conventional as well as nuclear, and aim at nothing less than the abolition of war as an institution, thus liberating energy and resources for peaceful development. But none of this will ever be possible unless there is a simultaneous and successive dismantling of national sovereignty as currently understood.

Thus, man may be at the beginning of a new stage of development in his incessant experimentation with forms of social organization. The many international organizations and supernational organs that have come into being since the end of the corporal's war all can be regarded as signs of a preliminary recognition that the national attitude, "enough unto oneself," no longer corresponds to the realities of our times. It may be that we can see in all this the beginning of a trend towards global organization of the community of men. The United Nations is a current necessity—but perhaps it is also a promise, an embryo, of something more, something stronger.

Considered realistically, the big powers' costly space programs ought to point in the same direction, even though no such trend can yet be detected. The prestige race to the moon, to which the competitors seemingly give a higher priority than they do to meeting many immediate human needs, should not be allowed to result in some nation's planting its flag up there and claiming "ownership," after the fashion of earlier centuries of predatory expansion. The very idea of a war over the Borrower of Light would seem to belong to science fiction at its most vulgar level. The reasonable course from the first day a man sets foot up there would be to consider joint administration of the earth's satellite—no matter what the nationality of the first man on the moon. Just as naturally, exploration of our closest neighbors in the planetary system ought to be a collective task for the scientists of the world. Is it utopian to think that such cooperation in space might open up new perspectives that could make it somewhat easier for us to reach agreements in some of our terrestrial affairs?

Whatever trends we think we discern, or hope to, there should be no illusions about any royal road to a world community. A great deal of further social experimentation will certainly be required, and there will almost certainly be numerous relapses into obsolete patterns of thought. Sometimes one wonders whether we must pass through a crisis that takes mankind to the very brink of the abyss, in order for sane men to be able to collect their wits.

It is vain to speculate about how a world government had best be structured if Utopia ever becomes reality. That will be a task for the social architects and social engineers of tomorrow. But it does seem more than likely that no effective global authority will be modeled on the present-day administrations of national states, and that it will have to be shaped in a quite different and more complex pattern.

One thing is certain: no world community will ever realize the dreams of a millenium. Our Odyssey will never lead to a Scheria. The cost of the security that a higher form of organization provides must always be paid for by loss of original liberty. Such is the case even in the world of atoms, and the world of man is no exception. In this case the price may come very high indeed.

We can venture a few plausible guesses about just how high the price will be if we visualize, albeit crudely and gropingly, the principal functions a world government would have to perform. Its primary task must obviously be to assume control of forces whose use or misuse can determine the destiny of mankind; this task is as self-evident as the fact that a world government must have a police force to control uncooperative communities. Even now, applied nuclear physics is under government control everywhere in the world. Though the justification for such control has so far been based on considerations of national defense, its acceptance represents a recognition that in dealing with the enormous forces that can be called forth from matter, there is no longer room for individual experiments. Transferring control from the separate states to a world-wide authority would mean only accepting the ultimate conclusion to be drawn from this recognition.

The other fundamental task of world government—one probably far more difficult of attainment—must be some kind of world-wide control over the use of natural resources. The dangerous exploitation and partial destruction by individuals and communities of natural resources, which will be regarded in tomorrow's world as common property of the human community, can hardly be permitted in a well-organized world community. A world government will have to draw up a global plan for the proper utilization of the earth's resources and determine certain limits that may not be exceeded. That is, it must draft a global ecological budget, one based on our best information concerning the world's land, forests, and water. If such a budget is to be balanced, total outgo cannot be permitted to exceed nature's capacity for renewal.

By and large, world government may become an anonymous technocracy that strictly rations global resources of food and raw materials. What the consequences may be for the rich and wasteful nations we can only vaguely surmise. In the rich countries, the counterpart of the population explosion in the poor countries is what Julian Huxley has aptly called the "consumption explosion." It has created artificial standards to support it because it is self-consuming and because it must be paid for by others to a considerable extent. To a world newly made aware of its own poverty, it must appear intolerable. If a world government tries to create some measure of global equality—another task so fundamental as to make it almost unthinkable that a world government would not have this clearly stated aim—then the world's upper class nations will surely be faced with demands that will be painful to meet.

Obviously, a world government cannot content itself with administering the globe just as it is. Progressively, it must improve human conditions and environment within the framework of the laws of nature by restoring the disrupted balance to the extent that it is possible to do so. What is needed is to repair some of what the sanguine centuries have destroyed—to restore to the land some of its original fertility, to grow forests (particularly at the sources of rivers), to clean up waterways, to check the spreading of poisons in nature and the pollution of the air. It will probably also become necessary to stop the wasteful use of newly created substances that have become part of our economy and are important for the processes of renewal. Where the ecological balance cannot be restored to its original natural state, it will be necessary to find artificial ways and means, and of course there will be the never-ending task of finding new sources of nourishment.

Even so, no attempt to create balance between world resources and human consumption will have much meaning unless the population problem is tackled at the same time. It remains the backdrop against which all other problems stand in bold relief. To the extent that it is a question of space, sparsely populated regions may be faced with the demand —the demand, not the request—that they open their doors to people from tightly packed areas and allow for regulated migration as a peaceful alternative to the assault of some latter-day Attila which population pressure would otherwise precipitate.

Getting to the root of the problem will require the restriction of population growth itself. In one way or another, a globally directed population policy may force itself on the world—a policy based on a balance sheet showing, on the one hand, what the globe can produce by way of vital food-stuffs and desirable commodities, and on the other hand, the maximum number of people which this shred of space can reasonably be expected to harbor, according to certain established criteria.

At what point such a global balance will be established will depend on what conditions man wants to grant to himself—on his criteria for material and cultural standards, on his requirements by way of elbowroom. If man is content to vegetate and to accept the ever more suffocating climate of overcrowding, perhaps those optimists are right who calculate that the globe is capable of feeding fifty billion people. But if it is decided that the optimum number of people to be housed on the earth should be determined, not in niggardly terms of material subsistence, but with due regard to the possibilities of the individual to develop—more precisely: what man, with his deep ties to the emotions of the age of the hunter, needs of living space in order to remain in reasonable harmony with himself and his environment—well then, we may already be very close to the maximum or even beyond it.

At whatever level we elect to make ends meet, we cannot avoid the need to create effective checks on our own proliferation—unless, of course, we blindly accept the chaos into which the Malthusian formula would otherwise lead us sooner or later. Just as it has become our burden and our adventurous opportunity, alone among the living creatures of the planet, to create a social organization based not on instincts but on conscious planning, so we are now forced to take our fate in our own hands and limit the growth of our species. Once we have torn down the fences built into the process of natural selection, we are forced into some kind of artificial quantitative selection. That having been admitted, can we exclude the possibility that a future generation will also try *qualitative* selection, in an effort to prevent the further deterioration of the species as a result of our random forwarding of the hereditary mass—the cry in the wilderness of today's eugenics movement? Since the process of natural selection no longer effectively weeds out what is seriously defective and perhaps unsuitable for life, can it then be assumed that man himself, organized into a world community, will never seek to take the place of the laws of nature in this respect also?

In point of fact, it can be argued that such a managed population policy, in its quantitative and, possibly, its qualitative aspects as well, would not be essentially different from the managed limitation and breeding of the other living creatures that man has brought under the management of his brain. But it would mean an interference with the freedom of the individual to a degree that has hitherto been approached nowhere on earth except in Japan during the harsh feudal centuries.

No matter how we ponder the functions of a world government, we always reach a point at which we have to acknowledge that the enormous, intertwined problems which tower over the path of man's future can probably not be solved through a new social organization alone. The question of our concepts and ideas again forces itself upon us. If the tensions within a global community are not to become

190

excessive, it must be supported by a system of ideas based on a fresh view of ourselves and our surroundings. Will it even be possible to erect the skeleton of the organization that will be required to meet radically changed conditions before we have subjected our own concepts and values to equally fundamental change?

To plan and act globally, we must perceive and think globally. An obstacle to be overcome is tradition—environment. One's view of the world is formed by the cultural environment in which one grows up. The environment's legacy to the individual is a set of ideas, concepts, and values that have been passed from generation to generation with relatively slight modification. Every social organization, every cultural unit, bases its existence on an awareness of a common past.

Until now our ideas about the past have been largely determined by regional perspectives and values. What we have been calling "world history" has actually been no more than regional history, different for different cultural units. The world history of the western world has been based largely on events in our own cultural sector and has been an expression of our ideas and evaluations, while other cultures have been regarded, as a rule, in the light of our accidental contacts with them, which have too often been those of the conqueror or the colonizer.

To plan for the future it is necessary to see the present against the backdrop of the past. For us to be able to plan for a global future it is surely of fundamental importance that our backward looks give us a total, global picture of man in time and space. The new totality created so recently by science and technology requires as its complement a view of history that takes into account the sum total of the significant aspirations, the ideas, the attempts at organization, the triumphs and failures, of mankind as a whole.

In such a perspective many previous judgments will have

to be reconsidered. Much of that which regional history has dealt with will erode and be covered by the sands of time, like a Roman triumphal arch in the African dunes. To the Chinese and the Nigerians, for example, the battles of Thermopylae, Pharsalos, and Trafalgar must be matters of monumental indifference. Strictly speaking, did most of these battles, cultivated by a durable tradition, have any *real* importance for western man? They were, after all, no more than flecks of foam on the wave of development.

If the past is regarded in total perspective, the long prehistory of man is likely to appear more important than most of what came to be preserved on clay tablets and parchment scrolls after man started to note down what he considered essential in a limited environment and a narrow span of time—more important if for no other reason than the fact that prehistory is common to *all* human beings, in *all* societies, at *all* cultural levels, and important also because prehistory explains so much of the later activity of man. With prehistory as the point of departure, it should be natural to see the continued path of man through the world against the background of the total environment of which he is part and which he himself has largely made what it is—to read history, in other words, not so much in the way it has been preserved piecemeal on clay and parchment, but rather as it has been carved into the globe itself.

Such a view of history is a natural foundation for ecology, this new discipline that tries to map the balance of nature and some day must come to be regarded as one of the most important of the sciences and the most elementary of the subjects to be taught in our schools. History and ecology merge, the past enters into the present. We see ourselves, not as isolated figures on a stage, but in relation to the earth we have impoverished, the forests we have devastated, the waters we have wasted and dirtied.

Perhaps such a perspective will make it easier to accept the restraints that man will need to impose on himself if he is ever to regain his balance with the environment.

But beyond that we may need something more, something touching the very heart of our philosophies.

In the last generation alone, man's unending and avid search has improved our knowledge of ourselves and the universe more than was done in all the earlier history of mankind—no matter how much remains unknown, perhaps unknowable. Science has not only yielded a clearer picture of the processes of evolution that have led to ourselves and of the relationships in nature. It has also opened up the cosmic expanses to our gaze, it has pushed ajar the door to the workshop of creation, it has permitted us to get a glimpse of the primordial elements out of which everything, energy and matter, life and nonlife, is built.

All of this has come with bewildering speed, and our knowledge still appears to be fragmentary. The layman, trying as best he can to find his way in the new dimensions, feels a powerful need for a synthesis that will permit knowledge of ourselves and our world—prcduced separately by astronomy and nuclear physics, biology and ecology—to merge into a total picture of man in the dizzying totality of time and space.

Even what we see in fragments is overwhelming. As we look towards the horizons spreading before us, we see ourselves as participants in a giant play of balances, in which our coactors are the microbes of the earth and the galaxies of space. We find ourselves players in a drama to which we have been called, not by sudden fiat to the vain task of dominating everything else, but borne on a planetary wave of evolution in intimate cohesion with all that our spatial fragment possesses of life—to this moment and to this spot. We have the overwhelming experience of being allowed—made as we are of the stuff of which stars are made—to glimmer for an instant in a continuous creation, never begun, never to end.

The picture of the world that is now unfolding for us must make many of our ideas wobble at their very foundation. Most of what we have called the "universal" philosophies have consisted of partial philosophies, the one vying with the other and all of them dispersing some of our best abilities. Just as sovereign national states have become obsolete in a world that can be circled in an hour and a half by man's new vehicles, so have most of our explanations of the world and our systems of faith become inadequate—formulated as they were in terms of a quite different picture of the world than our own and within separate cultural communities of which some have ceased to exist. The vacuum that has been created, between traditions frozen inside a vanished picture of the world and our new knowledge of the universe and ourselves, needs to be filled with a more realistic philosophy of the world—a philosophy that is consistent with what we can observe and know, or at least believe.

Our new picture of the world has no room for static concepts and rigid faiths. It has no room for notions of the transcendental or the absolute. This does not mean that we have to sluff off the experience gained from the old faiths or the wisdom embedded in the old systems of thought. Man's views of man are also subject to the law of evolution. As a rule they change as slowly as the position of the North Star, but in times when the search for knowledge opens new horizons, they must also adapt themselves to new facts—no matter how reluctant their interpreters may be to bow to the new.

Seen in the perspective of man's evolution, the various systems of faith appear as explanations of the world that are peculiar to specific times and environments. Where observation ceased, myth was allowed to embroider, and thus mythologies were the natural forerunners of intellectual systems of thought. It is possible to see the dominant religious myths as a symbolic language used in an attempt to explain the inexplicable and, in a way, not essentially different from the symbolic languages which scientists must use in visualizing what our senses cannot capture. What remains as a kernel inside the shell of the ancient myths must be regarded as something beyond everyday experience—man's feeling of awe before the enormous and his sense of merging into something larger than the individual self.

The gods of man have always been a transitory lot, and many of them have been extinguished like animal species that vanished when their time was up. If we melt down the surviving tribal gods and replace them with a cosmic-biological sense of life—an outlook that permits us to accept humbly our modest role in the totality while at the same time filling us with respect before the great event of our being part of this totality—a sense of the divine experience itself remains, but in a new dimension.

It is possible to regard the great political ideologies, which have attempted to rally man's creative forces around common goals, as secular counterparts of the religious faiths. The ideologies have also had their myths—what else was Rousseau's "social contract" or Marx' depiction of the "class struggle" except symbolic language seeking to describe man as a social being? In forms appropriate to their time, they articulated some of the yearnings of man. They promised no new heavens but they did dream of a new earth.

Words wear out and dry up, and one should perhaps be wary of thinking of the conceptual system called forth by a new picture of the world as some kind of secular religion or as an ideology founded on scientific "fact." What occurs to a wanderer on an evening by the sea, as he lets his thoughts rove around the world his companion will encounter, is that we need to gather all that our search in various fields has revealed to us into a vision of our own

195

destiny, one which may better equip us to face a future filled with dark menace but abounding in opportunities. Such a total vision might give us some of the wisdom that is so urgently needed in an evil time—for what is wisdom if not a controlling, total grasp of the sum of knowledge that man happens to possess at a given moment?

Looking at one's own experience in the double perspective—through one end of the spy-glass the individual striving to realize his personal goals of life, through the other end the human abode far out at the edge of a galaxy in a universe full of opportunities for life—all ambitions for national prestige must be reduced to petty incidentals. Globalism in thought and feeling should supply the construction materials needed to build a global society of men.

We shall have to put aside our cherished illusions. Behind us, no Paradise Lost; ahead, no Scheria. The heroism required of us is to accept this world as it is and to make the best of it.

This world—for no matter how many billions of light years our cyclops' eyes may permit us to peer into space or to what distant ports our space ships may soar, it is to this small speck that we were tied forever when the first protoplasm took form in the primordial sea.

The swell has subsided into a whisper barely heard. Soon another day will have exhausted its opportunities. Over a rocky isle, where two wanderers have found a resting place for the night, nature arches her mighty vault.

Nature is there—beyond our streets and houses, more or less near, more or less distant—and we are part of it; we cannot tear ourselves out of its totality without something breaking into pieces. We have tried it; we have believed ourselves capable of whipping nature into obedience, and with what ominous results!

Accepting the world as it is means, in the final analysis,

returning to the nature out of which we have come, not in the naïve way of Rousseau, but by trying to find again— while taking into account all the modifications made necessary by our civilization—that which corresponds to our deepest biological needs and, by cooperating with it, to shape our existence in obedience to the laws of nature. We must make peace with the natural forces on the surface of the earth if we are ever to make peace within our own species.

Socially, a global institution striving to create workable relationships between mankind and the individual; individually, a new attitude inside the horizons opened by fresh knowledge—both of these things appear to be equally essential to man's preservation and development of community in his marginal home between the cosmic realms of death.

The task is enormous. It may have to be accomplished within the next generation. Will that generation be capable of mobilizing the wisdom and heroism which we ourselves have been unable to muster?

My companion has risen to his feet. He casts a final glance toward the sea before turning to go down to the boat.

The rim of the sea rises slowly, devouring the sun.

The screech of the gulls is sharp and shrill.

Bibliographical Note

This list of readings, like that accompanying the original Swedish work, is limited to works that are accessible to the general reader. The German and Swedish titles have been deleted, and no attempt has been made to list the many United Nations publications from which information was obtained. On the other hand, a number of relevant titles published since 1966 have been added.

Ardrey, Robert: *African Genesis* (New York, 1961) and *Territorial Imperative: A Personal Inquiry into the Animal Origins of Property and Nations* (New York, 1966); Asimov, Isaac: *The Double Planet* (New York, 1960).

Benoit, Emile, ed.: *Disarmament and World Economic Interdependence* (New York, 1967); Bibby, Geoffrey: *Four Thousand Years Ago* (New York, 1961) and *The Testimony of the Spade* (New York, 1956); Borgström, Georg: *Hungry Planet* (New York, 1965); Boschke, F. L.: *Creation Still Goes On* (New York, 1964); Bracher, M. C.: *SRO, Overpopulation* and *You* (Philadelphia, 1966); Brennan, Donald G., ed.: *Arms Control, Disarmament and National Security* (New York, 1961).

Calder, Ritchie: *After the Seventh Day* (New York, 1961) and *Common Sense about a Starving World* (New York, 1961); Carson, Rachel: *Silent Spring* (New York, 1962); de Castro, Josué: *The Geography of Hunger* (Boston, 1952) and *The Black Book of Hunger* (New York, 1968); Clark, Colin: *Population Growth and Land Use* (New York, 1967); Clark, Grahame: *Archaeology and Society* (New York, 1961); Clarke, Robin: *The Silent Weapons* (New York, 1969); Cochrane, Willard W.: *The World Food Problem* (New York, 1969); Conant, James B.: *Modern Society and Modern Man* (New York, 1952); Coon, Carleton S.: *The Story of Man* (New York, 1954) and *The Origin of Races* (New York, 1962).

Dart, Reymand A., and Dennis Craig: *Adventures with the Missing Link* (New York, 1959); Darwin, Sir Charles G.: *The Next Million Years* (London, 1953); Dubos, René: *Men, Medicine and Environment* (New York, 1969) and *So Human an Animal* (New York, 1969); Dumont, René, and Bernard Rosier: *The Hungry Future* (New York, 1969).

Eiseley, Loren: *The Immense Journey* (New York, 1957), *Darwin's Century: Evolution and the Man Who Discovered It* (New

York, 1958), *The Firmament of Time* (New York, 1960), and *The Unexpected Universe* (New York, 1969).

Fromm, Erich: *May May Prevail* (New York, 1961); Fryklund, Richard: *100 Million Lives* (New York, 1962).

Gamow, George: *The Creation of the Universe* (New York, 1961); Grossman, M. L., Shelly Grossman, and J. N. Hamlet: *Our Vanishing Wilderness* (New York, 1969).

Halle, Louis J.: *Men and Nations* (Princeton, N. J., 1962); Harrison, George Russell: *The Role of Science in Our Modern World* (New York, 1961); Hawkes, Jacquetta: *Man and the Sun* (New York, 1962); Hoyle, Fred: *The Nature of the Universe* (New York, 1960); Huxley, Aldous: *Brave New World Revisited* (New York, 1958); Huxley, Julian: *Essays of a Humanist* (New York, 1964); Hyans, E.: *Soil and Civilization* (New York, 1952).

Kahn, Herman: *On Thermonuclear War* (Princeton, N. J., 1960); Kefitz, Nathan, and Wilhelm Flieger: *World Population: An Analysis of Vital Data* (Chicago, 1968); Kissinger, Henry A.: *The Necessity for Choice* (New York, 1961) and *Nuclear Weapons and Foreign Policy* (New York, 1957).

Laffin, John: *Hunger to Come* (New York, 1966); Lapp, Ralph E.: *Kill and Overkill* (New York, 1962); Leakey, L. B. S.: *Olduvai Gorge* (Cambridge, 1962); Libby, Daniel H., ed.: *Life or Death· Ethics and Options* (Seattle, Wash, 1969); Lovell, A. C. B.: *The Individual and the Universe* (New York, 1958).

Mellanby, Keith: *Pesticides and Pollution* (New York, 1968); Melman, Seymour: *The Peace Race* (New York, 1961); Milne, Lorus J. and Margery: *The Balance of Nature* (New York, 1961) and *Patterns of Survival* (New York, 1967); Moore, Patrick, and Francis Jackson: *Life in the Universe* (New York, 1962); Mudd, Stuart, ed.: *Population Crisis and the Use of World Resources* (New York, 1965); Myrdal, Gunnar: *Population, a Problem for Democracy* (Magnolia, Mass., n.d.).

Nam, C. B.: *Population and Society* (New York, 1968).

Osborn, Fairfield: *Our Plundered Planet* (Boston, 1949).

Pauling, Linus: *No More War!* (New York, 1962); Pfeiffer, John E.: *From Galaxies to Man* (New York, 1959) and *The Origin of Modern Man* (New York, 1969).

Rudd, Robert L.: *Pesticides and the Living Landscape* (Madison, Wis., 1964); Russell, Bertrand: *Common Sense and Nuclear Warfare* (New York, 1959) and *Has Man a Future?* (New York, 1962); Russell, Sir E. J.: *World Population and World Food Supplies* (New York, 1961).

Shapley, Harlow: *Of Stars and Men* (Boston, 1964); Stockwell, E. G.: *Population and People* (Chicago, 1968); Strachey, John: *On the Prevention of War* (New York, 1963).

Taylor, Gordon R.: *The Biological Time Bomb* (New York, 1969); Toynbee, Arnold J.: *Democracy in the Atomic Age* (Melbourne, 1957).

Wendt, Herbert: *In Search of Adam* (New York, 1959) and *The Sex Life of the Animals* (New York, 1965).